TEACHING YOUR CHILD ABOUT GOD

CLAUDIA ROYAL

Teaching Your Child About God

FLEMING H. REVELL COMPANY

Westwood, New Jersey
London E.C.4—29 Ludgate Hill
Glasgow C.2—229 Bothwell Street

Library of Congress Catalog Card Number: 60-8458

Printed in the United States of America

1.1

To

Elizabeth and Eugene

Preface

Dear Parent,

It has been a joy to work with you and your child. Your loving care and concern for him has been an inspiration to me. You have asked for help in answering his questions about God. That is the reason for this book.

From observation and study, from experiences with our own children in the home and others in church and school, a philosophy of childhood has evolved. This we share with you.

First, we look at the young child himself, that we may follow his bent in teaching him about God. Then we view the problems that hinder his upward reach and suggest ways of solving them. Finally, goals are set up and methods for attaining them are discussed.

We hope to challenge you with the truth that the young child can be guided in his search for God and to help you in doing just that. A list of books is provided for those who wish to do further research.

As you enter upon this happy journey with your young child, may you know the fulness of His love who said, "Suffer little children to come unto me. . ." (Luke 18:16).

Blessings on you!

Claudia Royal

MILL VALLEY, CALIFORNIA

Contents

TEACHING YOUR CHILD ABOUT GOD

CHAPTER ONE

Parents Are the First Teachers

Lo, children are an heritage of the Lord . . . (Psalm 127:3).

Parents are the most powerful people in the whole wide world! To them, God has entrusted the immortal lives of young children. To children, parents are all-wise and all-powerful. The young child thinks his parents can do anything. He is dependent upon them for his every need. They are, in truth, his very world.

Parents are powerful people because they have the first opportunity to create an environment for the best development of their children; to provide the basic needs of the child for personality growth: the need for love, the need for security, and the need to feel important. It is the feeling of things that counts; the happy and sad experiences that give rich meaning to life. Children need to feel that they are special, and beloved—to their parents! They inhale the very atmosphere of their surroundings!

At the heart of his being lies the emotional life of the child. Long before he speaks or understands the spoken word, he feels and senses attitudes. That is why the atmosphere provided by parents is so important. The greatest contribution that can be made to the child's life is an environment of love and security.

Psychologists tell us that the early years are the most formative period of life, that the child's future is determined largely by these early influences. His outlook upon life, his estimate of true values, his religious attitudes and experiences are all influenced by his parents. This is the time when impressions go deep. Dr. Hymes says, ". . . if any years have a very special importance, it is those long years before school begins, way back in early childhood. Those baby years when youngsters are just getting their initial impression of this world." [1]

The first and most enduring ideas of God come from parents. Impressions are made even in the first weeks and months of life. As the baby observes the parents at prayer, day after day, feels the atmosphere of reverence, and sees the expression on their faces, there comes an influence for God. As he grows a little older, he can kneel beside the parents and express his own simple prayer. There can be a meaningful song, and the quiet of the prayer time can make an ever deepening impression on his young life.

Every child has a right to learn about God, beginning in infancy. Just as he has a right to learn about the world into which he is born and the culture in which he lives, so he has a right to know about his spiritual heritage. In truth, in America such knowledge is a part of his culture.

Spiritual knowledge is necessary to the wholeness of life. The spiritual is an integral part of the young child. Much emphasis has been given to his physical and emotional needs. Volumes have been written concerning his care. Pediatricians, psychologists, welfare workers, and others offer their services to him. Yet all too often the spiritual life is overlooked. This should not be. There are spiritual laws that govern the development of his soul just as there are physical laws that govern the growth of his body. As the body must have food for growth so the soul must have spiritual nourishment for development.

God wants to make Himself known to the child, even at this early age. He uses human instrumentality to do this. Jesus showed the Father's concern for young children when He identified Himself with them. "And he took a child, and set him in the midst of them: and when he had taken him in his arms, he said unto them, Whosoever shall receive one of such children in my name, receiveth me. . . ." (Mark 9:36-37).

God allows parents to be the first teachers. The child's first and most intimate relationships are with his parents. The child learns nearly all he knows in these early years, from his parents and his family. Parents are potent teachers; they stand in the place of God for the young child. Faith of a child in his parents lays the foundation for faith in God.

Many parents of today have a religious heritage from their parents. Now it is up to them to pass on this spiritual inheritance. Spiritual capital must be renewed, else it becomes depleted. One generation cannot live on another generation's faith; each must experience God for itself.

Parents have a moral obligation to teach their children. The writer of Proverbs admonishes, "Train up a child in the way he should go: and when he is old he will not depart from it" (Proverbs 22:6). Parents can count on this promise. It never fails. Some may cite instances of failure but when investigation is made it is found that there were inconsistencies in the training. The parents had taught one thing and lived another; or they were faithful in church attendance but critical of church leaders; or they taught love for races of other lands but were unjust to minority groups in their homeland.

Some parents put off this teaching, having the mistaken notion that this spiritual development can be postponed until the child is older. This cannot be done, any more than the growth of muscles or the development of the nervous system can be postponed. The child formulates some theory concerning the cause of things as evidenced by his questioning. Christian teaching cannot be neglected until the child is four or five years old without permanent loss. He acquires some philosophy of life, even if parents refrain from teaching about God. A refusal to answer his questions does not stop the child's thinking. He gets ideas from his associates and his environment.

Jesus knew that many were indifferent to the needs of little children, and that some would even dare to hinder their religious development. In their mad desire for prominence and power, even the early disciples forgot their responsibility to children. To these followers Jesus gave this warning, "But whoso shall offend one of these little ones which believe in me, it were better for him that a millstone were hanged about his neck, and that he were drowned in the depth of the sea" (Matthew 18:6).

Parents teach whether they will or not. Their very lives make an impression either for or against God. This unconscious teaching—by the words they say and the things they do—gives the young child deep feelings which grow into attitudes toward the Christian religion.

God has commanded, "You shall therefore lay up these words of mine in your heart and in your soul . . . And you shall teach them to your children, talking of them when you are sitting in your house, and when you are walking by the way, and when you lie down, and when you rise" (Deuteronomy 11:18,19, RSV).

The home offers a choice classroom for teaching the Christian religion. It can be a ready-made laboratory for experiencing God. Parents can make the home what they want it to be. In it they can place the best in literature, the finest in art reproductions, and most important of all, the ideals of Christianity. The home then becomes a place for the young child to learn about life.

Parents who provide a truly Christian home give to their children a happy and secure childhood. Happiness in childhood makes for well-adjusted adulthood. Psychologists maintain that many maladjustments of adult life can be traced to unfortunate and unhappy experiences in the early years. No amount of wealth, power, or fame in later life can compensate for a barren, loveless childhood. Conversely, no adult can have a richer heritage than the memory and influence of a happy childhood spent in a home with Christian parents, where he learned early of a loving Father God who cares for all people.

At the heart of the home is the mother. She has the closest contacts with the young child. She has the first and largest opportunity to meet his physical and emotional needs. She can give guidance in spiritual growth. The feeling of security she provides is a basis for that growth.

Three-year-old Joan had just finished her prayer and jumped into bed. As her mother tucked in the covers she inquired, "Does God love me more than *you,* mummy?"

"Yes, He loves you more than I ever could," was the mother's reply. "Then He must love me lots," contentedly sighed Joan as she settled down for sleep.

One can be the best mother only when she is a dedicated Christian. A mother needs to know God as well as pedagogy. Back of Moses was a God-fearing mother; back of Samuel was Hannah. History reveals that mothers have stood back of the great leaders of all time. Truly the destiny of our country lies far more in the hands of mothers than in the hands of lawmakers.

Out of her deepening experience with God the mother teaches her young child. Within each life she finds possibilities for good: the young child's soul reaching out toward a Father God. The mother gently guides in that search.

Joy was only eleven months old when her mother started a devotional period with her, preceding the morning nap. She read short verses from the Bible and explained their meaning. She told the little daughter about God's love and then the mother said "thank you" to God for all His gifts. Ten months from the time this altar of worship was established, little Joy said one morning, "Mommie, I wanta talk to God." The mother was so amazed that her twenty-one-month-old daughter wanted to pray that she just sat there and looked at her. Surprised at her mother's hesitancy the infant girl said, "Well, close your eyes and bow your head." Then came a prayer from her child's heart, "T'ank you God for Daddy. Amen." [2]

If mothers are to guide their children in experiences with God, they must be willing to do a lot of "mothering." Just old-fashioned, honest-to-goodness cuddling and loving. Mothering of the baby has a direct relationship to his feeling of security, which is the foundation for feeling the love of God, for his ability to make mature emotional relationships in adult life. The baby's personality has an emotional hunger for mothering just as his body hungers for food. He needs to be caressed and fondled, talked to and sung to. He comes to feel important and wanted. Thus, his personality unfolds and glows!

Working mothers find it difficult to give time and energy for this mothering. They cannot give themselves to their little ones as they ought. When they arrive home they are all spent; they have little energy left to enjoy loving experiences with their children. The young child becomes clinging and irritable. He cries when the mother goes out of sight. He is afraid of losing his mother. Mothers need to stay home with young children. Spock believes, "It would save money in the end if the government paid a comfortable allowance to all mothers (of young children) who would otherwise be compelled to work." [3] Many illustrations could be given to show the wisdom of these words. One will suffice.

Mary was a healthy baby who seemed to enjoy life the livelong day. She was the youngest of three children and her parents were devoted to their little family. The mother gave of herself to her children, telling them stories, answering their questions, planning picnics and excursions. Then, one day, family fun was disrupted. Mother had to go to work. The father was most cooperative and tried to share the home chores and family responsibilities, but he was a busy person, too, with a job and studies at school. Mary became upset, fearful and unhappy. She cried when her mother left and demanded to sit in her lap when her mother was home. Being a conscientious person, Mary's mother became frustrated and confused. A happy home life was sacrificed and the present and future tranquility of the children was jeopardized.

Many mothers do not feel the need to work. They find life's greatest fulfilment in their family. Homemaking becomes a career. The greatest career in all the world is motherhood! Many young mothers are gloriously giving of themselves in this their chosen career. Truly, "the hand that rocks the cradle rules the world."

The wife of evangelist Billy Graham was quoted by a newspaper: "Some women feel frustrated if they can't have a career but not me. Frankly, I feel sorry for those who must go out and work, because being a mother is the most wonderful life in the world." Mrs. Graham is the attractive mother of three girls and two boys.

Father is the other member of the team. He has a part in teaching his young child about God. When a child has a warm, understanding father, it is much easier to teach him about a loving Father God. Being a dad is the most challenging experience a man can have! Life takes on new meaning when a young fellow hears that baby utter his first word, "da, da, da!" New zest comes into his work; he looks forward to a home-coming at which tiny arms entwine about his neck.

Roy was such a young father. There were two children in the family: a two-year-old boy and a four-year-old girl. When their afternoon naps were over, the two kept watch at the front window with fond anticipation awaiting daddy's home-coming. When he arrived each vied with the other to give him a "bear hug and a big kiss." No wonder that father was a happy, useful man.

If father and children are to have a warm relationship,

they must have many happy experiences together. This requires parental cooperation. Many mothers arrange the home schedule so that the father has time with his children. Children need their father and a father needs his children.

Fourteen-month-old Jean Carole was a happy baby. For her, strangers soon became friends. Her day usually went well until late afternoon. Quite often this was a time of fretfulness. That is, until she heard her daddy at the foot of the stairs as he sounded out in his deep, bass voice: "Jean! Jean! hello!" Immediately a smile covered her face and she kicked her feet in glee. Dad was home and all was right with her world!

Father is important to his child. He needs to give of himself to his little one. What he does *with* his child is far more important than what he does *for* him. Companionship with his father gives a child a feeling of togetherness and belonging. Four-year-old David expressed it this way: "I don't know what God looks like but I think he must look like my daddy!"

These truths are sometimes overlooked because of the pressure on the father of providing for the material needs of his family. Father thinks he will get ahead while his children are small. Later, when he is freer of financial worries he will spend more time with his children. That day never comes. Responsibilities increase and ambition grows. Children grow up without knowing their father. He is that stranger they see on weekends, the man who pays the bills. That sense of security father thought to establish is lost in the mad rush of climbing the ladder of fame and fortune. When the children have left the home for life on their own perhaps he may ask: "Why didn't someone tell me life was passing me by?" He has cheated himself as well as his family. The early years offer the father a golden opportunity to contribute to the child's life and to gain an intimate fellowship with him that will bear rich fruitage in the years ahead. Every man can be a success as a father.

The father has a special place in the family. He is a representative of God, invested by Him with the responsibility of governing the home and leading in the religious training of the children. "And, ye fathers . . . bring them up in the nurture and admonition of the Lord" (Ephesians 6:4).

In the early Jewish family, the father's first responsibility was for the religious training of his child. He accepted it and passed on the heritage of his race. During colonial days in this country the father was closely associated with the child. By example as well as by precept, the young child learned from his father the tenets of the Christian faith. Today, there is danger that the economic pressure and ambition for advancement will cheat the child of his rightful place with the father. In far too many homes the father has no time nor inclination to lead in the religious life of his family.

In the days of the judges Samson's father prayed, ". . . O my Lord, let the man of God which thou didst send come again unto us, and teach us what we shall do unto the child that shall be born" (Judges 13:8). In the days of here and now, the father of little children can look to the minister of God to show him what he is to do for his little ones. This minister of God will point him to the church. Parents need the assistance of the church in giving spiritual guidance to little children. Members of the family need to go to church together. Father must lead in this. When he goes, the children want to go. Although the church can never be a substitute for the home, it has something to offer that the child cannot receive elsewhere. When children develop a love for the church in these early years they remain loyal to it in later years.

Faithful, participating parents reap their reward when in later childhood and adolescent years their children accept Jesus as Lord of their lives and become devoted members of their church. Such parents take courage in the growing faith of their children. They rejoice in victories won in young lives. Their hearts are grateful as they watch their children grow into strong Christian citizens.

Parents have within their power good guidance of young lives that are to make the world of tomorrow. They can provide a home environment where the child knows he is loved, where he feels important, and where he learns of a God of love. Parents have the power to choose a church where the teachings of the home can be reenforced. They have the rare privilege of walking the high road of faith in the happy companionship of their children.

CHAPTER TWO

Young Children Are Like That—Nursery Age

And they came with haste, and found
. . . the babe lying in a manger
(Luke 2:16).

Jean Carole was five days old and she was going home from the hospital. Grandfather and grandmother were waiting for her father to bring her down. Flitting through their minds were many questions. Who does she look like? What color of eyes does she have? Will she like us? When the blanket was turned back, grandparents looked into the big blue eyes of an adorable baby! Jean Carole nestled in her mother's arms with implicit trust.

Babies are like that. They are altogether dependent upon their families. They trust their loved ones.

There was a time when the first two years of life were not considered so important to character building. It was thought that the infant's paramount need was physical care. Proper diet, correct amount of sleep, plenty of sunshine and cod-liver oil are essential to character building, because a healthy body is essential. The healthy body grows rapidly. This physical growth can be related to his spiritual development. The baby's feeding time, spent in his mother's arms, gives him a feeling of belonging. As she cooperates with him in his basic needs and individual urges, she finds the baby developing a spirit of cooperation. When he is loved and his physical needs are properly provided for, the baby is generally healthy and makes adjustments to life. He is happy and receptive to spiritual influences.

However, there are many requirements other than the physical if a proper foundation for later Christian character is to be laid. Dr. Britt, the social psychologist, tells us, "When it comes to attitude development or personality characteristics, the sorts of behavior that surround the child in his first few months and years may have far-reaching effects." [1]

The spiritual environment in the home—the values of life and the family patterns of conduct—all have an influence upon this baby. Never again—while habits are unfixed, and unpatterned emotional behavior is easily modified—will the child be so pliable in the hands of those who would guide him. Jean Carole's parents know that what they do with their baby in the first two or three years of her life will determine to a large degree what she will do and be in the later years of her life.

Growth of the normal baby is uniform. His emotional and mental powers develop as his physical body grows. As these three phases mature, he also becomes more social minded. All four aspects of development are tied together and should move forward simultaneously. It is essential that we understand these aspects and their relation to each other in order to guide the spiritual development of the child. As we supply the baby's physical needs we give him a feeling of being loved. Such consideration provides a sense of security, which has much to do with his spiritual growth.

Every baby has his personal pattern of growth, his own rate of speed. It is unfair to expect one child to advance according to another's style of progress. Each has a personality all his own; each is different. This is evident to the mother at the age of *one day!*

However, there are characteristics common to each age group. A knowledge of these characteristics will help us to work *with* the child and not *against* him in this matter of growth. "We need to remember that a baby is born with certain capacities for growth."[2] Ours is the privilege of guiding that growth.

For the sake of clarity we shall divide the years of early childhood into four periods: Infancy (up to the second birthday), the two-year-old, the three-year-old, and the kindergarten age (four- and five-year olds). Each period of life is related to the preceding period and to the period that follows. One merges into the other. Many characteristics continue from one age to the next. Some traits are only "growing phases" and are left off at the next stage. Only by knowing what has gone before can we understand the child at any age level.

Infancy (Birth to Two)

BABIES ARE DEPENDENT AND TRUSTFUL

Waking from her afternoon nap, six-month-old Marla Fay smiled engagingly and kicked her feet in glee. With her gurgling and cooing she seemed to say, "What a good world this is!" When mother came to take her up, Marla Fay went to her with utmost confidence.

An evident characteristic of the baby is his utter dependence upon others. God has a purpose in making this little one dependent upon his parents and loved ones. As the baby learns to trust them, so he can later learn to trust and rely on a loving Father God. Herein lies the opportunity to teach him the meaning of love and faith.

A baby needs a lot of loving. Mrs. Anna Wolf, on the staff of the Child Study Association of America, tells of an experience in a babies' hospital.[3] The infants were given the best possible physical care. Every precaution was taken to keep them from disease; the slightest defect was corrected immediately. In spite of this expert clinical care these babies suffered in comparison with babies who lived at home and came to the clinic for occasional checkups. Although these other babies were brought up under adverse circumstances, some of them even in tenement districts, the "home grown" babies were more robust physically and showed greater mental alertness. Physicians, puzzling over the contrast, decided to experiment. On each hospital baby's chart was written this instruction: "One hour of loving a day." After only a brief period these institutional babies showed marked improvement.

THE BABY IS AN INDIVIDUALIST

He struggles when his arms or legs are restrained. These protective measures reveal the deeply rooted need of even the infant to manifest his own individuality. This characteristic, properly guided, develops into self-respect and strength of character so necessary for the Christian life.

The baby needs time for spontaneous play and development of his own initiative.

Parents need to allow for individualism in children. Children have a right to their special likes and dislikes. If a child has a retiring personality, parents should respect it and not push him into activities or rush him with strangers. The truth is that strangers easily make a friend of a young child as they follow his lead and let him make the advance.

Eleven-month-old Daniel was just such an individualist. He did not like one of his mother's friends. He tolerated her at a distance but when she approached him, he started chattering in a loud voice and then started crying. No one knew why he disliked her. Daniel was reticent about meeting people. When a stranger came to the home, Danny played in the kitchen until he had become more accustomed to the person, and then made his appearance. If rushed by a person, he clung to his mother or father until the person left him alone.

THE BABY IS IMITATIVE AND PLASTIC

Jean Carole's father had the habit of whistling as he went about the house. One morning, three-month-old Jean Carole made a new, peculiar sound. When her mother went to her crib, she found her baby drawing air in and out through her puckered lips as she tried to whistle like her daddy!

The baby is imitative. He imitates the sounds he hears, the facial expressions he sees, and the emotions he feels. This places a grave responsibility on parents. The baby unconsciously reproduces their emotional and mental attitudes. If parents are calm and happy the baby naturally grows into a calm and happy child. If parents are reverent toward God the child feels it.

BABIES LIKE TO BE NEAR PEOPLE

Even though babies are very active and are constantly on the move—after they learn to crawl and walk—they want to know that parents are in the vicinity. Out-of-sight and out-of-sound means out-of-their-world to them. In their waking hours, they seem to feel rejected when they are left alone for long periods of time; personality seems to be dwarfed and there is a lack of spontaneity and joy in the baby's expression.

Provide a play area within eye-reach and ear-sound. Your baby will be happy and you will have peace of mind. Take time for a word with him occasionally. You strengthen the bond of comradeship with him. Take him with you to the grocery store or to the neighbor's house for a brief playtime with another baby. Take him to the church nursery. After he becomes acquainted, he will enjoy being there. Here he can play with other babies. He learns that people at the church love him and that it is a happy place to be. The church is set to reenforce the teaching of the home. Never mind if the nursery is not what you think it ought to be. Band together with other parents to make it so. The experience will bless you as well as your baby.

BABIES ARE EAGER TO FIND OUT ABOUT THEIR WORLD

That is why they are into everything! They take things apart just to see what makes them tick. They pull things from the bureau drawer; they feel, smell, and taste whatever they can get their hands on. This is the baby's way of learning. This knowledge is essential to his adjustment to the world in which he lives.

BABIES ARE CONSTANTLY ACTIVE

Perhaps the most noticeable characteristic of infancy is activity. The baby is never still; even when he sleeps he moves. To remain still for more than a few minutes at a time is a physical impossibility. Growth is so rapid that his body literally demands constant exercise. "A baby may be expected to double his birth weight during the first five or six months." [4] As his body grows he learns to sit upright, and later he begins to walk. His activity then becomes more obvious.

Eighteen-month-old Patsy was a lovable little girl. Her eyes saw everything. Her ears heard everything. Tiny little hands clutched everything. Things dropped very easily, but by using all her fingers Patsy retrieved them. Walking, and a slight bit of running ever so often were fun, but so was the odd bit of crawling which she did with adeptness. She seemed to give the impression that the floor felt good as she slid over it on her knees. Sitting down was all right, but only for a brief time.

Patsy was constantly on the move, traveling from one object to another, with no set pattern, repeating over and over the same circuit. Brightly colored pegs attracted her. It was fun trying to put them inside the plastic jar but it was more fun to hear them rattle around in the jar. Only a few moments passed and she noticed a linen nursery rhyme picture book on the table. Pegs were forgotten and she walked across the room to the table. Clutching the book with both hands she turned around for approval.

When she saw her mother's smile she walked around a bit before she sat on the floor, where she looked at and touched the colored pictures.

Wooops! Patsy heard something—the sound of a rocking chair. Over she went with arms raised, asking to be lifted up and rocked. Rocking was fun, but only for a moment. What's that she saw? A rabbit on the book shelf. Down she climbed and over she went to see the rabbit. She was too short. Back she came for help. She was lifted up, felt the toy and heard her mother call it "bunny." Down she went again. Bang! She stumbled over something—her pegs. Again she played with them, for a little while. And so it went. The routine was repeated over and over. Now and then she went over to her mother for a smile of approval and then she was off again. Patsy seemed to have perpetual motion.

These first two years present many opportunities for parents. As they learn what their babies are like they come to understand their needs and try to meet them. They are glad for the privilege of parenthood and for every occasion to encourage an environment of love in the home.

The baby absorbs the spiritual atmosphere about him and is affected by it equally as much as his body is affected by the air and sunshine that surround it. Guidance in spiritual development must begin in infancy. Teaching the child about God can begin in babyhood and can be a continuous, joyous experience. To this end, suggestions are given in chapters six and seven of this book.

The Two-Year-Old

Louise Woodcock[5] has given a most charming picture of the two-year-old. She has presented the child of this age with a personality and development all his own, which sets him apart from other age levels. Books such as hers are a source of instruction and inspiration.

The two-year-old is in a transition stage from babyhood to childhood. No longer is he the dependent infant who must rely on adults to meet his every need. He has learned to walk and is rapidly learning to talk. However, many of the characteristics of infancy are carried over into this new stage of growth. As parents teach him about God, they need to know what the two-year-old is like. The following traits give a brief view of him.

ACTIVITY

Like the infant, the two-year-old is constantly moving. Sometimes he lugs about play equipment that is much too heavy for him. His muscles seem to cry out for activity and he seems to be in a race to catch up with the months when he could neither walk nor run. This urgent need for movement necessitates a short attention span.

The two-year-old will stand on the fringe of an activity and observe older children in cooperative play. Occasionally, he may spontaneously plunge into the play but only for a moment. Louise Woodcock tells us that, "he maintains a touch-and-go relation to his whole environment." [6] The two-year-old goes happily on his way, first with one interest and then with another. He likes to know that others are nearby but he wants to explore on his own. He has no time nor inclination to team up with them.

Ronald was a lovable two-year-old who spent most of his waking hours exploring. He had two loves. One was a family of kittens. He never tired of carrying the babies to their mother and then away again. The other love was to imitate his father, especially in the carpenter and repair work his father did in his spare time. His father, a mechanic on an ocean liner, was a bit careless about putting away his tools, so his young son carried away the hammer and as many nails as he could find to "fix" the fence, his wagon, or even the cats. Ronald seemed to have an unusual mechanical interest and it was amazing how quickly he could unlock gates and doors.

Give this two-year-old plenty of space to run and play. Give him as much freedom as he can safely use.

IDENTIFICATION OF HIS OWN PERSONALITY

As the two-year-old's horizon enlarges and he makes friends outside the home, he becomes conscious of his own personality. He begins to identify himself as separate and apart from others. He is important to himself!

There are reasons for his recognition of self-hood. He has learned to walk and has become a "runabout." He is beginning to have better use of his body because of improved coordination. He is beginning to talk and can assert himself. In short, he is becoming aware that he is somebody!

Parents do well to recognize this young self-hood. Accept him as an individual. Respect his personality and treat him as "somebody." He is ready for a room of his own with low shelves for his toys and low hangers for his clothes. He will not take over the care of his possessions but he will begin to help. When he says "me do it," let him. Be not concerned with how he does it, but be concerned that he has the satisfaction of doing it.

GROWTH IN POWER OF EXPRESSION

The two-year-old is more aware of his surroundings and his vocabulary is increasing, so that he can more easily express his thoughts. A child of this age can begin to voice his own simple prayer as he is led at mother's knee. He is old enough to enjoy short Bible stories told in his own language. He can learn about his friend Jesus as he looks at pictures of the Friend of children.

The two-year-old is talkative. He talks to himself; he does not need an audience. Through trial and error he learns the correct word to express his thoughts.

Dian was the two-year-old daughter of a Chinese merchant. When there were guests in the home she liked to listen to their conversation. Once in a while she picked up sentences from the adults and practiced them on her four-year-old brother or her small friends. She talked with expression on her face, using her hands and shaking her head like the adults. Although she had to learn both English and Chinese and had difficulty with "th" and "r," she never gave up. Talking was fun to Dian!

A DISCOVERER

As with the infant, the two-year-old is a discoverer. He has a zest for life that leads him into new experiences. The world is an interesting place to him and he keeps busy exploring his small portion of it.

Lanny, a two-year-old, was down by the lake when rain began to fall upon the summer world. At first, he was disturbed. He looked at his hands where raindrops had spattered. Then he raised his arms to shoulder level and let the rain fall on them. Finally, he looked out over the lake and his troubled expression vanished. Slowly and softly came the word, "rain." A pause, and then again, exultingly, "rain." Lanny had discovered rain.[7] As Lanny discovers rain, he can be told that God sends the sunshine and the rain. Through the discovery of nature he can be led to a fuller knowledge of God.

POSSESSIVENESS

The two-year-old is possessive. He makes much use of the pronouns "me, my, mine." He is in the "me too" stage. He seems to think of everything and everybody with reference to himself. Sometimes he hides his toys when he leaves them, so that they will be waiting for him on his return. He will thank you to leave them alone!

NEGATIVISM

Somewhere along the way, when a two-year-old is growing toward three (sometimes before the age of two!), parents may have to deal with a stretch of negativism. This phase usually reaches a peak about the age of three. With an increasing awareness of his own personality the young child sometimes sets up a pattern of resistance. It may be that heretofore he has been cooperative and obedient. Suddenly, he develops an irresistible urge to test his power over others. The result is a consistent "no!" to every question and request. Sometimes he says "no" when he means "yes." This may be merely a way of asserting his independence.

Negativism should be considered a transitory stage through which the young child passes. It is so common that it may be considered normal. It need not unduly disturb parents. If handled wisely, the little individualist soon learns to cooperate with others.

Give him freedom in minor matters. When interference is necessary, be gentle with him. Don't hurry him—that tends only to tighten him up. Try to be understanding. When he must do things that seem unpleasant to him (such as taking out time for eating!) make a game of it. A little story with a jingle or a song (extemporaneous) helps a lot! Do not make an issue of a thing, just assume that he will do it—with you! As time goes on, he will learn a better way.

The Three-Year-Old

As the young child grows, his powers of perception increase. He is capable of receiving more from his environment. Life is unfolding new powers for the three-year-old. Though not so rapidly as the two-year-old, he continues to grow physically and by the end of the third year he may double his stature at birth.[8] There should be a corresponding emotional, mental, and social development. Parents need to have some understanding of his nature. Spiritual truths need to be adapted to the child's own nature.

Getting acquainted with the three-year-old is like meeting a charming new friend. He can carry on a conversation with you. As his body and mind have grown he has developed self-confidence. He is not quite so dependent as he was. He is leaving babyhood behind. He is emerging as a distinct personality. This little person has many characteristics that open the way for teaching about God.

PURPOSE IN ACTIVITIES

Unlike the two-year-old, who seems to be constantly busy just for the fun of moving, three-year-old children usually have purpose in their activities. They have acquired greater skill in motor coordination and they show this in their play life. They can build a simple house with blocks. They can draw circles. There seems to be design in their construction. Most three-year-olds have had enough sensory experiences to be ready to use materials for some constructive end. With this increased ability comes a desire to help. The three-year-old can do many things to help himself and others. This is the time for teaching him to take responsibility.

Let him do for himself. He wants to. Parents sin against a child when they do for him what he can do for himself. It takes more time and the job won't be done as well, but he grows thereby. It isn't efficiency but character development we're after at this stage of the game. Work and responsibility become desirable patterns when accepted at this early age.

"Now I am three, almost four. I'll soon be five. When I'm five I go to school," said Carol, as she talked with the visitor in her home. Carol also told this visiting lady about her big achievement. She baked a custard pie "all by myself but Dram-Ma helped." It was a good pie, too, and Carol had done everything except mix the dough!

The young child's spiritual life grows as he learns to do things for others. "We '. . . are helpers . . .' " (II Corinthians 1:24) is a fact that can be made very real to him at this age.

LEARNING TO PLAY WITH OTHERS

The three-year-old is more interested in playing with other children; not yet in large groups but with two or three, if you please. He cannot cope with many children but he does enjoy a few his own age. His interest quickly shifts from one group to another.

Richie was an energetic boy of three. He had a large back yard and the neighborhood children spent much time playing there. Richie liked to ride his tricycle and to play in the sand. He spent time with the other children but his playing was often independent although he was near the group.

Occasionally, a child of this age insists on being the leader at all times. He must be taught to take turns and to follow as well as lead. Out of his play experiences this little child can learn sharing and cooperation. "And be ye kind . . ." (Ephesians 4:32) can become meaningful to the three-year-old.

CURIOSITY

Like the elephant's child, who was full of " 'satiable curiosity," the child of three asks questions about everything he sees, hears, smells, tastes or feels. He is a quantitative question mark, and his curiosity drives him into all areas. This is the young child's way of learning new truths and it offers a genuine opportunity for Christian teaching. Many of his questions about God astound an adult. Most young children want to know, "Where is God?" "What does God look like?" Little Johnny asked, "Is there a Mrs. God?" The answers must come from a deep experience. One cannot share a faith he does not possess.

This inquisitiveness is God's way of providing growth for the young child. Wise is that parent who takes time for his child's questions, thus knitting more closely the bond of fellowship between them. Every question is an index finger pointing to a need and deserves a thoughtful and truthful answer. Answer his questions in language he will understand. Go from the known to the unknown.

Questions comprise a large per cent of the child's conversation. No longer is he content to learn about things merely through his sense of taste and touch. He takes a short cut and goes to adults to get his information about things he sees and hears.

Sometimes, parents have to say, "I don't know, but we'll look it up." Together, they do just that. They keep a book on nature-study handy for ready reference. A reliable standby is Comstock's *Handbook of Nature Study*.[9] For the child there are lovely picture books at the public library. A visit to the children's division is an excursion in itself!

Sometimes a young child asks a question that is hard to answer. He deserves an honest answer. Not long drawn out details. Just enough to satisfy him. When he is ready for more he will return. This question and answer activity can be an exciting adventure. It can draw parent and child into a purposeful partnership in quest of knowledge.

FRIENDLY TOWARD ADULTS

The three-year-old seems to like adults. He makes such a delightful friend! He pays an adult a high compliment when he accepts him as a friend.

This is an age when the child begins to admire his parents. He thinks they can do no wrong. He tries to be like them in looks, speech, and deeds. This devotion offers parents the opportunity to lead him in the way he should go. Spock tells us that his "feelings toward the parents aren't just friendly; they are warm and tender." [10] Many times the three-year-old reaches to adults beyond his family with his affection. This relationship can be very rewarding to the fortunate person.

Three-year-old Rudy was in his mother's office nearly every day but he was not acquainted with the "bookstore lady" next door. One morning the "bookstore lady" called to him but failed to get his attention. Then she noticed his cowboy boots. "Hopalong Cassidy, you want a ride?" she greeted. He seemed willing and she swung him round and round and up and down. After that, every time Rudy came in (and he came often now) he wanted a "cowboy ride."

Once his new found friend offered him a choice of her candy bars. After serious consideration he chose a "Mr. Goodbar." He was allowed to put the nickel in the cash register. Almost every day thereafter, Rudy came running (he never walked) into the store to "chat" with the "bookstore lady."

Winning the friendship of a three-year-old is an easy thing to do—if you get down on his level. And it gives rich returns—especially to the adult!

The child of nursery age has many character traits that open the way for teaching about God. He must be dealt with as an individual, in line with his personality. The more parents learn about him the better they understand his needs and recognize the possibilities of his young life.

CHAPTER THREE

Young Children Are Like That—Beginner Age

And the child grew, and waxed strong in spirit . . . (*Luke 1:80*).

As the child grows older individual traits become more pronounced. Some of the characteristics of previous years continue while others have almost vanished. The beginner is still active, but with more purpose. His trustfulness is a bit deliberate. He is less dependent upon others. Self-centeredness is gradually giving way to outgoing interest in others. He is still imitative and easily influenced. Negativism should have spent itself, yet there will be resistance to authority at times. He is still asking questions, but is able to find some of the answers for himself.

Most of the characteristics we attribute to four- and five-year-olds have their beginnings in earlier years. We say the young child is "growing up," but we must not make the mistake of expecting adult behavior from him. He is still a child. His religious nature, as well as his intellectual nature, will be expressed as a child. Often his simple faith in the goodness of God is superior and sweeter than that of the adult.

We must not "push" the child in teaching him about God. His religious concepts will be very childlike, not theological! Give him the truths of the Bible (which he can understand) but give them in his own language.

The child of this age must be taught according to his readiness. Paul said, "When I was a child, I spake as a child, I understood as a child, I thought as a child; but when I became a man, I put away childish things" (I Corinthians 13:11). No child should ever be hurried beyond his ability. Each has a rhythm pattern, a speed of his own. As he progresses from one age level to another, individual differences become more and more important. Study the child. Follow his lead!

The Four-Year-Old

Four has been spoken of as a "frustrating" age. It can be. The four-year-old wants to be out and doing on his own. He has his own friends now and likes to play with them.

Janet was Susie's best friend. Every morning while the older children were getting ready for school, there came a soft little knock at the door. There stood Janet. With eager eyes she inquired, "Can Susie come over and play with me?"

Fours enjoy being together. They talk and plan; boast and brag; and have a noisy good time. They are full of themselves and the fun of life. They have delightful times together until there comes a disagreement. Then comes name-calling and contention. There may be flying of fists and shedding of tears. Yes, the four-year-old can be frustrating!

Sometimes we are apt to expect too much of this "big little child." We want him to have adult manners. We are annoyed with his noise and rowdiness. Too many times the thing we consider wrong is just an inconvenience for us. At other times, we may think of the four-year-old as still a baby who must be near us all the time. We forget to begin "loosening the apron strings." We forget his need of a little more freedom for his growing independence.

At times Whallen is a frustrating four-year-old. The sound of his "stick 'em up, stick 'em up, bang, bang, bang!" can be heard daily. He is energetic and full of abandon. He is such a bundle of "rambunctiousness" that his mother (who is just recovering from an operation) finds it difficult to cope with him. Whallen is a "bright" boy and is a constant "chatterbox." When he enters a group there is never a dull moment.

The Five-Year-Old

Five marks an end to the period of early childhood. Five is a fascinating age. The five-year-old is usually a conformist. He wants to please. His increased vocabulary places his conversation more on the level of an adult. He delights to tell his parents about his day in kindergarten or his play with friends. Listening to him encourages him. He does not need speech errors corrected, now. He will learn correct speech as he hears it in the home. Let him enjoy the flavor of uninhibited talk!

The five-year-old likes to be trusted. Give him responsibility he can handle. Let him help about the place, even if he is slow and inefficient. He needs the satisfaction of accomplishment to build self-respect.

The five-year-old is a busy person. He has better use of his body, especially the large muscles. His interest span is increasing and he will stay with a project longer—if you get his attention!

Gale is a fascinating five-year-old. Brimful of vitality and free with her smiles, she wins the heart of all who see her. She is a "chubby" child, well built, with fair hair, blue eyes, and rosy cheeks. Her home atmosphere is pleasant and wholesome. She is a leader with other children. She plays dolls, skips rope, and is a master at "jacks." She has many books and likes to listen to stories. She loves babies and treats her kittens almost as tenderly as if they were human. She likes kindergarten very much. One day she was playing "funeral" with her friends. A plastic jewelry box contained the deceased—a twig. Said Gale, concerning the twig, "It's just sleepin'."

Characteristics Common to Fours and Fives

There are some characteristics common to both fours and fives. They seem to be distinctive at this age. A few are briefly discussed to show what these children are like.

IMAGINATIVE

The child of this age usually has a vivid imagination. He lives in a world apart—in the realm of "make-believe." He can "plike" (play like) he is a horse, a car, or a train, without the slightest stretch of the imagination.

This is the time when stories mean so much to him. He never tires of hearing them. He also likes to have picture books read to him. Through his imagination he enters into the lives of the story characters. On his magic carpet he sails to other lands and peoples. This keen imagination makes possible the formation of ideals that will guide him through life. Child-life stories, with positive patterns of behavior give him correct models. Stories of Jesus' love and helpfulness make him want to be like Him.

Sometimes, a child of this age has an imaginary playmate, especially if he is a lonely child. Upon the death of her mother, five-year-old Josephine came to live with her grandmother. All the children in this family were grown up. Josephine invented a play-like friend. All day, as she went about her play, she talked with her friend. When she served tea she would say, "Jane, won't you have a cup of tea with me?" So vivid was little Josephine's imagination that her friend seemed a reality. "Imaginary playmates are sometimes very real to children three years of age and older." [1]

Now, an imaginary friend can do no harm unless he becomes all absorbing. If left alone too much the imaginary friend draws the child into a world apart. This ought not to be. Josephine needed playmates her own age. She would have profited from kindergarten experience. When no kindergarten is available mothers can invite other children into the home. Other children in the family bring the closest companionship. Often an only child is a lonely child.

The church kindergarten is a good place for this age to find playmates. Here, they enjoy the companionship of other children. Here, they have happy associations under the supervision of adults who love them. Here, they learn about God and His love.

Another manifestation of his imagination is the fanciful story. Sometimes he tells tall tales! Listen to the tale and then let him know that you realize it is make-believe. "That was fun—your 'play-like story,'" you may say. Never tell a young child that his story is a lie. He does not yet distinguish between fact and fancy. Encourage his imagination but let him know that you do not accept "for real" the fanciful tale. Help him to see that the imaginary story is fancy.

LIKES DRAMATIC PLAY

Because he is imaginative, the child likes dramatic play. A stick becomes a horse, a bed becomes a boat, a chair becomes a train, anything at all becomes another thing through the magic of his imagination. Play is usually home-centered. One of his favorite activities is home-making. The girl is not always the mother; sometimes the boy acts the part. They love to play "tea party" and have mother visit them. The tea, sugar, and cream are all "make-believe" but seem very real to the children. They like to dress up in mother's high-heel slippers and in daddy's old clothes.

One morning in kindergarten the children were having a time of free play. They arranged the chairs in a double line for their "train." Four-year-old Mary Ann was among the passengers. A five-year-old boy was the conductor. When he came to Mary Ann she had no "ticket." When he insisted that she produce her ticket, she just sat. She gave no excuse nor would she leave the train. After the conductor passed her by, Mary Ann got off the train, got her ticket from her coat pocket and gave it to the conductor. The train continued on its way.

IMITATIVE

The young child is an imitator. He reflects the people and experiences with which he is surrounded. If he admires an individual he tries to be like that person.

Jeanette loved her church kindergarten teacher. For her she could do no wrong. She admired the way she dressed, the way she combed her hair, the way she talked. Two years later, even though Jeanette had not seen her teacher since kindergarten graduation, her mother reported that she still talked about Mrs. Robinson and tried to comb her hair like her.

It may be unconscious or it may be deliberate on the part of the child but day by day the process goes on. He must have models by which to chart his course. How important that he have the correct conduct patterns to imitate! What an opportunity and a responsibility for parents!

Jesus can be presented so vividly through story, song, picture, and life, that the young child will be constrained to imitate him. Dr. Hymes says, "He needs humans he truly likes as a pattern for himself. Youngsters look up all the time. They are searching for models they can shape themselves after." [2] Parents who follow Jesus present safe patterns for early conduct.

SELF-CONTROL AND SELF-RELIANCE

Fours and fives are growing in self-control and self-reliance. They can do many things the younger child cannot do. They have acquired greater skill in the use of the body because of finer motor coordination and increased mental ability. They should be encouraged to help, first by caring for their own needs, and then by assuming responsibility for small chores about the home. This develops self-reliance.

Five-year-old Sharon is the third of four children. She does not feel the pressure of being a "middle child." Each child is a vital part of the family. When mother bakes, Sharon is allowed to help. She makes small pies and cakes with the same ingredients. Sharon has her own electric iron and ironing board, and has learned to iron handkerchiefs and doll clothes. Her mother says, "Work turned out is not perfect, but it's good training for Sharon." Work is fun at this age. The young child who helps with the work of the home, feels more a part of the family.

Growth in self-reliance develops a desire for leadership. The child wants to lead the line of march, be the mother in the playhouse, or the engineer on the train. Occasion is offered for teaching children to take turns, and to show love and kindness for others.

The young child should be treated as an individual and should be shown the same courtesy that would be given to a stranger. Four-year-old Julia expressed it this way, "Please," she said to her mother, "play that I'm company and be nice to me."

The kindergarten child should be given as much freedom as he can use to develop self-reliance. A child who is too closely supervised will become too submissive. When parents make all his decisions for him, he fails to develop self-reliance and initiative.

Five-year-old Stephen showed unusual self-control and self-reliance. He had a younger brother. Stephen liked mechanical things. His favorite activity was making something with wood. Out in the yard he was always building something: a swing in the tree, a playhouse, or a kite. His father encouraged him and helped him. Stephen liked nature and liked to find out about little creatures. He often caught butterflies and bugs and put them into jars, which had holes in their lids. He liked to look at picture books and listen to stories. Animal and Bible stories were his favorites. He enjoyed cutting pictures out of magazines. He could carry on an intelligent conversation with an adult. Sometimes he told his mother something that was not true and then he said, "I wuz teasin'!"

Although he would rather play with other children, Stephen was satisfied at times to play alone. He liked to build with blocks and enjoyed finger-painting. Stephen was a well-adjusted five-year-old.

LITERAL-MINDED

The beginner is literal-minded. When he hears the story of "Jesus the Good Shepherd" he thinks of a shepherd out on the hillside with his sheep (if he is familiar with oriental customs). He does not think of Jesus caring for His little ones. He does not make the transition from the type to the concrete.

Children of beginner age do not understand symbolic expressions. For that reason children's stories must be of familiar things about the "here and now"; their Bible stories must be about experiences they can understand; their songs must be in simple language. Symbolism has no place with this age.

Little four-year-old John had just entered the church and was sitting by his mother. "Is God here?" he whispered. "Yes," answered the mother softly. Said John, "I didn't see his car outside when we came in."

Adults give children many false concepts by their use

of symbolic words and phrases. Carolyn was the five-year-old daughter of a student pastor. At the beginning of a Wednesday night service, her father called attention to a family who were moving away the next day. Said he, "I just know you are on needles and pins trying to get off." Carolyn raised up in her pew and gasped as she looked back at the family. When the service was over she went at once to her baby brother and inquired, "You're not on needles and pins, are you?"

In their minds we limit God when we speak of the church house as God's house. Rather we should say, "This is the church house, a special place where we learn about God." Our homes belong to God, too, and we want our children to think of Him there. Sunday should not be called God's day—other days belong to God, also. Sunday is a special day.

Children may hear symbolic terms in the hymns of worship, in the minister's message, and perhaps in other places. Do not let this worry you. They will come to you for explanation, if they are disturbed by them. Just be sure you do not use such terms yourself.

CAPACITY TO WONDER

Twinkle, twinkle, little star.
How I wonder what you are!
Up above the world so high,
Like a diamond in the sky.

One evening at dusk, four-year-old Elizabeth was walking down a village path with her hand in mother's. On the way home, stars appeared in the sky. "Mother," said Elizabeth, softly and reverently, "I wanta talk to God."

The little child has a capacity to wonder. Five-year-old

Norman expressed it thus, "God can do everything anybody can do!" This characteristic is revealed in the questions he asks about God and the beginning of things. The things of nature seem to bring a glow of wonder to his face.

In these early years, as he views God's handiwork, the young child can be led to think of God as a loving Father and Creator. The things of nature may inspire the first sense of wonder, and provide a direct pathway to God. Faithful and truthful answers to his "who" and "how" questions lay a foundation for a fuller understanding of God in later years.

Sometimes, we will have to say, "I don't know" or "I don't understand it, but this is what my Bible says." The Christian religion is based on faith as well as fact.

Clarence H. Benson[3] tells of a little boy who approached his father with the oft-repeated question, "Who made God?" The father's reply was, "No one made God, my boy. He always was." The child puzzled over the answer for awhile and then said, "He always was? I don't understand that." "Neither do I, son," answered the father frankly.

The young child's senses are keen and he perceives the beauties of the world about him. Much of the joy of life is lost to adults because they have ceased to be aware of little things. As the young child sees the wonders of nature, he can be told that God put them here to show His love. The beauties of nature call forth awe and reverence toward God when he is taught that "He hath made every thing beautiful in his time . . ." (Ecclesiastes 3:11).

Beautiful music and beautiful works of art inspire reverence and a sense of wonder on the part of some young children. Four-year-old Ralph was attending a morning worship service in a beautiful church building. The sun was streaming through a large stained glass window depicting Jesus kneeling in Gethsemane. On the front wall was a lovely large picture of Jesus. Ralph leaned over to his mother and whispered, "Mama, is this heaven?"

As parents look into the personality portraits of young children they tread on holy ground. God made them like that and He has given parents the privilege of working with Him to help each child achieve his best self. Children come to them with possibilities for both good and evil. Parents have the opportunity of laying the foundation for a good life, a life of happiness and usefulness.

Parents need to keep ever in mind that though they have many characteristics in common, each child is different and must be dealt with as an individual. Remember, too, that every phase of his life has a bearing on his religious development. This development can come only when religious truths are related to his everyday experiences in language he understands.

We have presented here a few facets of the young child's nature. There are many more. Seek them out. Study your child—be a companion to him—he will reveal his inner self. As you work with him, his characteristics and needs, you work with God. "We are laborers together with God."

CHAPTER FOUR

Living Is Learning—With Young Children (I)

. . . And learn from me; for I am gentle and lowly in heart . . . (*Matthew 11:29*, RSV).

"These are your happiest years," said an older friend to a young mother. "How can she say that?" thought the mother of two children, ages one and three. "I'm busy every minute, day in and day out, running this-way-and-that, with never enough time!"

Life with the young child is a busy time but it can be full and satisfying when we understand his nature and needs. Living happily with little children involves learning how to meet their everyday problems. In its beginning stage a problem can be more easily solved.

Now there are two ways of looking at the young child's problems. One is a morbid view, in which every slight misbehavior is attributed to some complex. Parents begin to worry and think of the problem as some moral perversion.

The other attitude, which Christian parents should have, is that problems reveal symptoms of maladjustment that loving care and patient guidance can remedy.

Usually, the problem is a temporary one. Some problems are aspects of normal growth. Others can develop into serious maladjustments. That is why parents need to face them and guide in their solution. Dr. Hymes says that "Every age of childhood has some smudges and rumpled spots."[1]

Just as the body must be healthy if the child is to grow physically, so the mind must be healthy if he is to grow spiritually. Body, mind, and spirit are inseparably linked together. A problem that affects one phase of life influences the other. All problems have some bearing on religious development. Because they are so closely related to his spiritual growth, some of the child's problems are briefly discussed in this chapter. Since they are such powerful factors in the little one's personality development, many chapters and even volumes could well be given to their consideration.

Parents should study the helpful books written for their guidance on these questions, being careful always to keep a Christian attitude toward the subject. We need to remember that perplexing problems can hinder the religious development of young children.

There are times when every child feels tensions. They seem to be a necessary part of growing up. These tensions can be handled when the child feels secure in his parents' love.

The Lord promises, "As one whom his mother comforteth, so will I comfort you" (Isaiah 66:13). The security we know as children of God is symbolized by the protection and care of loving parents.

Eating

Eating sometimes becomes a problem to parents, especially to the mother. She worries about the baby's refusal to take solids or the little child's lack of appetite. Consulting a doctor is the wise course when it becomes a serious matter.

Two-year-old Jane gave her mother much worry because she ate so little. She had no regular hours for meals. However, when she visited her next door neighbor she always climbed up on a stool and asked for food. Usually she ate quite well.

Many eating problems can be solved by a change of attitude on the part of parents. This is the time to show unconcern. A child will not be undernourished if he misses a meal or fails to eat a certain food. A healthy child will balance his diet over a period of time.

Do not nag. That only makes the child more stubborn. He sees that his resistance gets attention. He has found a way of asserting his independence—a source of power over parents. Let him miss the food or the meal, if need be. Never bribe. Avoid between-meal snacks and more than likely he will eat at the next meal. Adults need to remember that there are times when they do not care for food. So it is with the child. Never force the child to eat.

Introduce a new food when the child is hungry, before his appetite has been satisfied with familiar foods. Give him his meal in pleasant surroundings, away from distractions. Relax and enjoy the meal with your child. A mother's tension reacts on the child and the atmosphere becomes charged with emotion. Make mealtime a happy time of family togetherness. No nagging about table manners here, please. Manners are caught rather than taught. Stories, picture books, and tea parties for mother and child can aid in this teaching. Give meals a seasonal party atmosphere. Just simple things like a valentine tree and place cards, Lincoln logs, etc. Let the child help in planning for these festive occasions. Even the two-year-old can have a part in this preparation.

The best way to insure a happy mealtime is to recognize its spiritual significance. Even the baby senses the feeling of reverence and gratitude as a simple "thank you for the food" is said before meals. This is an opportune time to teach that God provides the food but He lets people help Him. A very helpful story, "Our Daily Bread," may be found in the Standard Bible Story Readers, Book One, by Lillie A. Faris. This introduces the child to the thought of God's provision for our needs.

Even an infant is impressed with the thanks for food. Seven-month-old Jean Carole was chattering and jingling her teething ring when the family sat down for a meal. As her father offered a prayer of thanks, she looked up at him and became still and quiet.

With proper management healthy children eat what they need. Parents' attitude toward food and mealtime are a determining factor in the matter. Keep mealtime routine. Plan pleasant experiences and expect cooperation from the children. "Children grow best when they look forward to coming to the family meal and enjoy not only the food but the companionship around the table." [2]

Sleeping

Sleeping can present a problem. For the first six months of life the baby spends most of his time sleeping. As he grows older life becomes more exciting and he hates to leave it.

Children vary in the amount of sleep they need. They seem to require more sleep in the winter than in the summer. Parents need to recognize individual differences. They must consider the sleep pattern of each child. There may be a variation from day to day, but over a period of time the healthy child usually gets the amount of sleep his body requires.

When the nursery age child stalls for time and tries to put off going to sleep, do not become upset. Keep bedtime at a regular hour. Allow no unavoidable variations. Give him a pleasant, clean room (his own) in which to sleep. Deal patiently but firmly with him. Expect him to sleep. Spock recommends that parents "have an air of cheerful certainty about it." [3]

After the child has gone to bed parents sometimes freely discuss unpleasant matters, assuming that he is asleep. *Never* discuss controversial matters within the child's hearing. He may not be able to hear distinctly but he senses tensions and lies awake building up anxieties. Avoid overstimulation during the day and especially just before bedtime. Even two- and three-year-old children are sometimes subjected to harrowing experiences with television, movies, and radio.

When parents are going out in the evening it is wise to have the babysitter come early enough to read a story or otherwise get acquainted with the child while they are still there. Prepare the child for the experience by "building up" the babysitter to him. If possible, keep the same person for a long time so that the child will not have to become acquainted with a new person each time. Never slip away. Always tell the child when you are going out. He will sleep better and will not wake frightened later in the night.

Refusing to sleep may be an attention getter. The child may be feeling insecure about something. Try to meet his need for attention in a legitimate way. A happy day is good insurance for a peaceful night. Avoid scoldings and tensions at bedtime. Ruth Strang says that "most of the bedtime battles between parent and child need not occur. Sleep is normal and necessary."[4] Never put the child to bed for punishment. We want him to think of going to bed as a satisfying experience.

At the age of two-and-a-half and sometimes earlier, the child usually builds up bedtime rituals. He wants to do the same things in the same way at the same time each night. Parents do well to recognize this trait and keep the matter of going to bed a simple, unhurried affair. Do not allow the ritual to become too elaborate. Remember this ritualism is a passing phase. By the age of three, the child usually leaves off a lot of stalling. Going to bed seems to be easier for him then.

Bedtime offers a golden opportunity for spiritual development. This can be a time of very warm and responsive relationships. One mother planned for a story-hour at the close of the day. As the two children gathered in the living room with their parents, father read to the children, one sitting on each knee. The children were allowed to choose their favorite books. After the picture-book reading came a Bible story suited to the two-year-old boy and the four-year-old girl. At the close of the story the family knelt for prayer. Each child voiced his own prayer of praise and petition. It was simple but in faith. The children went to bed with the thought of God watching over them during the night.

Make the going to bed a pleasant time at the end of the day. If the little girl wants her favorite doll let her take it to bed with her. If the little boy desires his teddy bear allow him to have it. Speak words of encouragement and endearment to your children as they lie down to sleep. Remember that the last waking thoughts work on their subconscious. The last impressions of the day should be those of peace and joy. As the little ones come to trust the loving care of their parents, so they can be taught to trust the watch-care of an all-loving Father God.

Anger and Temper Tantrums

Anger is an emotion that all people have to deal with. When it comes in a stormy outburst we call it a temper tantrum. Now an occasional temper tantrum during the first two or three years of life is nothing to be alarmed about. When it continues into the fourth and fifth years as a regular thing, it becomes a matter of deep concern.

The little baby has his every wish cared for. As he grows older and his environment enlarges he meets obstacles. These he attempts to remove and when he can't he feels frustrated and angry. He sometimes becomes explosive and "goes to pieces." When people get in his way he treats them as things and lashes out at them. Sometimes he loses control in a "fit of anger." If temper tantrums continue beyond childhood, it is usually because of defective training. It is up to parents to establish controls for the child until he is able to do it for himself. The child likes to know that there are limits to which he can go.

Parents must get at the root of the matter. It takes insight, courage, and patience to recognize the cause of such outbursts. The tendency is to meet anger with anger and punish the child severely. This loses the battle for both parent and child. Usually a cross, irritable child is not well. An ugly attitude on the part of a child who is ordinarily loving and cooperative is usually an indication that his physical condition is not normal. Lack of sleep or improper diet may be at the root of the matter. Perhaps he has been overstimulated by frightful television programs or horrible motion pictures. It may be that he has been kept up at night for the convenience of parents.

When the child expresses anger in the form of a temper tantrum there is always an underlying cause. It may be that he has a nervous disposition and has resorted to this form of behavior to gain his own way. Do not give in to him. He will have to learn to cope with frustrations in life. He cannot always have his own way. "The child has to learn to do what goes against his wishes occasionally, to abandon a cherished plan if it interferes with somebody else's well-being." [5] If we give him what he wants when he throws a tantrum he has succeeded. He will repeat the process.

Whenever possible, temper outbursts should be prevented. Unnecessary thwartings should be avoided. Don't expect too much of young children. Paul's admonition applies to parents today, "And ye fathers, provoke not your children to wrath: but bring them up in the nurture and admonition of the Lord" (Ephesians 6:4).

Give him a place of his own where he can enjoy unrestricted play. A part of his play (as much as possible) should be out-of-doors in a safe area within view and calling distance. Provide materials for constructive activity.

Be not overexacting in your requirements. Keep a routine for meals and bedtime but give freedom in minor matters. In a routine matter do not ask if he wants to do it but calmly assist him in doing it. He feels more secure when there is regularity to his day and he knows you are in control. When you must call him from some absorbing activity, give him a few minutes warning. Divert his attention with some toy or experience. Use as few "no-no's" and "don'ts" as possible. When you say "no" or "don't" you make a thing more inviting.

Help the child when things seem impossible for him. Just enough to get him over the hump. Not enough to stifle initiative. Thus you help him acquire a sense of achievement rather than a sense of frustration and failure. Encourage him to undertake projects within his ability. When accidents happen such as falling down or knocking into something, help him to assume responsibility for his blunder. Do not blame the floor or the chair. Even a little child can face reality.

Avoid criticizing or unnecessarily crossing the little child when he is hungry or sleepy. Many little children need a glass of juice or some light nourishment between meals. Especially is this true if they play out-of-doors. Blatz and Bott tell of an experience in St. George's Nursery School.[6] The children spent the first two morning hours in outdoor play. Then they came indoors for an hour's play before dinner. Most of the outbursts of anger came at this period. The routine was changed and the children were given orange juice when they came in from the playground. The display of temper was appreciably reduced.

A calm climate in the home is the best insurance against temper tantrums. When parents control their temper, they encourage children to do so. A relaxed atmosphere is conducive to cheerful children. Once the temper tantrum has become established as a habit there is no one certain cure for it. There are many ways of dealing with it to help the child establish control. What the Bible says is true: "A soft answer turneth away wrath . . ." (Proverbs 15:1). The parents' calm, kindly voice can help a child control his temper. An angry child must be dealt with firmly but patiently and considerately.

Jimmie lost his father when he was just a baby. A few years later his mother married again. The new father, in service for his country, was reported "missing in action." His mother became upset and tense with her child. Jimmie began to "throw fits of temper." He became unmanageable. The grandmother took over. When Jimmie had a temper tantrum she calmly but firmly sent him into a room alone. Here he sat in a big chair. His grandmother always said, "You don't act like you feel well. You need to be by yourself for awhile. When you are able to be around people, you may leave the chair." Little Jimmie took some time to get himself under control. Finally, he called out, "Nanna, I'll be good. Can I come out now?" After several isolation experiences, Jimmie gave up his temper tantrums and took on better behavior.

Usually, a temper tantrum will not continue if the child is ignored and he sees that he gains nothing. He should be removed from the presence of others and allowed to have it out by himself. Sometimes, a child may have such a violent outburst of temper that he makes himself sick. Emotional upsets can be very devastating to a young child. Treat him as if he were ill. When the tantrum has subsided, give him a warm bath. This will help him relax and then he is ready for rest and perhaps a nap in a quiet, darkened room.

When the temper tantrum is over and the child is calm, talk with him about the matter. Reassure him of your love. He thinks he has been such a "stinker" that no one loves him any more; you can let him know that you love him, even though you do not approve his action. Remember that when he is the most unlovely that is the time he needs your love the most. Let him know that you, too, have a struggle to control your temper. Talk with him about finding a better way. Show him how foolish temper tantrums are; that they get him nowhere, only making him and others unhappy. Let him know that it takes a strong person to control temper.

This is the time for talking with our Father God. The young child can be led to see that God understands and forgives, when he is sorry, and will help him to do better next time. Remind him, however, that he must cooperate with God by doing what he can for himself. Encourage each step of progress. Be patient and loving with him as he endeavors to overcome the habit of hot temper. As you help him to control his anger you will be growing in self-control!

Negativism

The outstanding characteristic of three-year-old Richie was negativism. He constantly said "no" and meant it. He was very stubborn and often seemed to want to do the wrong thing just to see how others would respond. He sometimes asserted his independence by being destructive. When he was having ice cream in the home of a friend, Richie suddenly said, "I'm going to tear this plastic tablecloth!" Although he tried to make the friend think he was going to do so he did not tear the cloth. Richie seemed to be an unhappy child. He had an older brother with whom he tried to keep pace. He seemed to feel inferior because he could not do everything his brother did. He had temper tantrums on occasion.

This type of behavior is so usual that we have already mentioned it as a trait of the two- to three-year-old. When this "developmental phase" grows into unhealthy hostility and unreasonable resistance it becomes a problem. If handled unwisely it may continue into later childhood and an attitude of contrariness may "pervade the whole personality."

Resistant or negative behavior may become a pattern when the little child finds it necessary continually to protect himself against outside interference and coercion. It can become a fixed habit if parents do not help the child to outgrow it. Parents who are too permissive sometimes allow negativism to become a perplexing problem. When parents throw up their hands and say, "I can't do a thing with him!" they are inviting tyrannical behavior. Blatz and Bott tell us that "the negativistic attitude in children calls for attention and discretion because it reaches to the roots of personality and may leave lasting effects unless corrected." [7]

Regimentation is another cause of negativism. The overdirected child either becomes too submissive or he builds up attitudes of negativism. The more he is ordered about, the stronger his emotional reactions become.

Give him opportunities to build up his self-respect and self-confidence through constructive channels. That is what he is after! He has been resisting authority to show that he is somebody and that he has rights, too! Provide plenty of free play with constructive materials. Give him little chores about the house; make him feel a part of the family. Furnish his room with low shelves and low hooks so that he may look after his own possessions. One of his objectives, though he may not realize it, is to get greater control of his own world.

Sometimes a child will be stubborn with one parent because he knows he can get by with it. He has measured that parent and found him lacking in firmness and consistency. On the other hand he may cooperate with the other parent, whom he has learned will carry through a request. He soon discovers how far he can go with different individuals.

Association with other children may help to solve the problem of negativism. The child will gain much from a good nursery school. He comes to have a feeling for others that may help him leave off negative ways. It is easier for him to conform when he is a part of a cooperative group. Mrs. Stern, director of the Castle School, tells of an experience like that.[8]

Four-year-old Bobby had two older stepsisters at home and had acquired the philosophy, "You have to fight for your rights." When he came to the Castle Nursery School, two-year-old Harry clung to him for protection. Bobby acquired a protective attitude toward the younger boy. When the little fellow cried for his bed at home, Bobby brought him toy after toy until his crying stopped. Then Bobby reported to the teacher, with deep satisfaction, "Mrs. Stern, it's teddy bears he likes best."

In breaking down the habit of negativism try to secure the cooperation of the child. See that meeting requirements brings satisfaction. Avoid direct commands. When he is in a good humor, talk it over with him and try to show him how to handle his emotional resistance. Remember that negativism is just strong will turned in the wrong direction. Our aim should be not to crush the strong will but to turn it to constructive ends; to help the child establish inner controls.

Aggressiveness

Negativism, temper tantrums, and aggressiveness are related problems. Just as with temper tantrums, it is expected that the young child will show some aggressive action. When such action becomes habitual it may be termed a problem.

"Aggressiveness should not be treated as a temporary behavior problem that will disappear by itself." [9] It requires parental action. Parents must teach the little child that *his* freedom ends where the *other* person's freedom begins. That he has no right to interfere with the rights of others. They should teach their children that life will, of necessity, bring some frustrations. Teach them how to take them in stride, how to bend to circumstances without breaking.

The child wants to be controlled. He does not want to be a "bad" child. When parents help him to control his aggressive impulses he gets a feeling of accomplishment and pride in achievement. If we are to help the child learn control of aggression, we must look for the underlying cause. Sometimes, he has been mismanaged in the home.

Four-year-old John was the oldest of three children. His mother, the oldest of five, had always felt that her mother expected too much of her and didn't love her as much as she did the others. She determined that John should not suffer the same fate. She allowed him to have his own way at all times. One summer she took her family to her mother's home for a long vacation. Immediately John staged a shouting and stamping show, which amused his mother. He destroyed a typewriter, papers, and whatever was handy. He seemed to delight in doing things he was told not to do. His mother never corrected him when he took things from his little sister, but simply found something else for her. Naturally, his grandparents became annoyed with him. Also, he was a very unhappy child.

Sometimes, a young child acquires the habit of aggression by watching older children use the same techniques. In this case he needs to be separated from that group. Playing with older children puts him to a disadvantage and encourages his domineering tendencies. Acts of aggression seem to make some children feel *big*. Said four-year-old Tommy, "Look at me! I'm tough! I can beat 'em up. I'm a *big* guy!"

An aggressive child may charge into a group, letting his fists fly for lack of knowing a better way to make friends. We must help him to see that "good" conduct wins friends, while hitting and kicking make enemies. Some children are overly aggressive because they feel unloved and unwanted. They need extra love and attention. They need reassurance of parental love. The neighborhood bully may be such a child.

One day five-year-old Ned came running home to his mother with a bloody nose. When Mrs. Abernathy investigated she found a new child, Ronnie, in the community who appeared to be a bully. She visited the new neighbors. Ronnie's mother had only condemnation for her small son. Mrs. Abernathy decided to experiment. When she took her son on an excursion, the "bully" was invited to go along. Ronnie's mother reluctantly gave permission with the warning, "He'll spoil your fun." After a few experiences like this, Ronnie's mother decided that her boy must not be so bad after all; that if other people thought he was so fine, then there must be some good about him. Gradually, her attitude changed and Ronnie's behavior showed corresponding improvement.

We would not eradicate aggressiveness. A strong drive is an asset in this competitive world. Like anger, it needs to be directed to constructive ends. Give the child legitimate ways to work off steam: clay to pound, balls to throw, blocks to build, and nails to hammer. Keep him busy. Let him help with the gardening. Digging provides a wonderful outlet.

Art also offers an avenue for expressing feelings. Every home needs an easel and water paints where the little child may express himself. Finger paints are fun, too. Music furnishes another medium. A drum, a triangle or a tambourine encourage the little child to express his feelings. As he grows older he will learn rhythm. All these media have value for the hostile child only as you allow him free expression. Do not circumscribe him with directions!

Sometimes, an aggressive child may need to be removed from a group. He may require individual therapy. We must teach him a better way from the beginning. Get him to talk about it. It may be that he can rid himself of some of his resentment as he talks it out. Read to him the Bible teaching on the matter: "A man that hath friends must show himself friendly . . ." (Proverbs 18:24). Explain to him the meaning of the verse: that the best way to make friends is to be friendly; being kind to his playmates and doing helpful things will show that he wants to be their friend. Plan with the child some act of kindness for a playmate, thus helping him to experience the Bible verse. Tell him stories of friendly children. Let him know that you understand how he feels, but that you can't let him run roughshod over other people. Encourage him as he tries to make improvement. Let him know that you are on his side, as he works at the job of self-control. Gradually, you will find him cooperating with you. You will be glad that you strengthened his strong will and helped to direct it into healthy habits.

Jealousy

A child's aggressiveness may be an expression of jealousy, as when he attacks the new baby. Jealousy is the hidden cause of many conflicts in early childhood. Many young children are plagued with this green-eyed monster.

During early childhood jealousy usually appears when a new brother or sister comes into the home. This antagonism has sometimes resulted in bodily injury to the baby. The older child feels that the baby has usurped his place and he would like to be rid of him. One child asked, "When are we going to take him back?" "The child may assume a martyr's role and brood upon the unfairness of his plight." [10] He may revert to baby ways. Sometimes he becomes boisterous or in some other way tries to attract attention. He feels insecure and unloved. Three-year-old Kenny lived on a farm. When his baby brother arrived he wanted to know if he could trade him off for two goats. Kenny demanded attention and when he didn't get it at once he fell on the floor kicking and screaming.

Jealousy may take another turn when a new baby arrives. It may cause the older child to be very protective. Elizabeth was twenty-seven months old when her little brother Eugene came. From the time that she first saw him in the hospital she was radiantly possessive in her attitude toward the baby. Naturally, the parents were proud of their young son and would show him to their friends, explaining that his name was Eugene. On one occasion the little sister was heard to exclaim, "No! Not *you*-Gene—*My*-Gene!"

Do not expect to prevent or eradicate all jealousy. You will be disappointed if you do. However, there are many things that can help. Parents can do much to avoid this jealous attitude. Prepare the older child for the coming of a baby by telling him about it ahead of time. A month or two in advance is long enough. The young child has little notion of time and he finds it hard to wait. Provide ways for him to help in getting ready for the new baby. When purchases are made take him on the shopping tour and give him a voice in the selections. Include something for him now and then. If this is impractical, at least show him your purchases and let him help in putting them away. Make him feel that "it" is his baby, too. A happy anticipation of the baby's arrival can forestall morbid jealousy. As the little child works with the mother she can bring him to love the expected baby. The event will then bring happiness to all the family.

If he must give up his room or his crib for the new baby, do this several months ahead of time. Do not wait until the baby comes home from the hospital and the older child has so many other adjustments to make. Project it as a promotion. You may say, "Now that you are such a big boy, you can have a larger room and a larger bed." Help him take pride in his new quarters. Add some new creative material to his play equipment.

Plan well in advance for the hospital stay. If possible keep the older child in his own home with his daddy and some trusted helper while you are away. Prepare a little note (including pictures!) to leave for him, in case you must go to the hospital in the middle of the night. Let him visit you in the hospital whenever this is allowed. If he can only wave to his mother through a window, that will help. At any rate he can talk with her on the telephone. A picture post card from "Mommy" will be treasured also. All of this requires forethought but it pays in peace of mind for the mother and happiness for the young child.

Then comes the time for the new baby to arrive home. Perhaps it will be well to allow the young child to go on an excursion on that day. After the new baby has been settled in his home environment and does not require so much attention (for the moment!) he can return home and find the baby. Have a gift for him and give him special attention at this time.

It is hard for the young child to share his parents with the new baby. To him, his parents are the most important people in the world. Be gentle and patient with him until he gets used to the idea. Find time and ways to show him you love him even when the baby is taking so much time and devotion. Make him feel sure of your affection. Then he will not need to work for it.

If your child is jealous, accept it. Tell him that children

often feel that way toward a new baby. Explain to him why he feels that way. Let him know that you have enough love for both. Explain to him that God has entrusted the new baby to him and that the Father is pleased when he helps with the baby's care. Stress God's love for all children.

Fathers can be a great help in this matter by giving more attention to the older child at this time. Let him feel that he is even more important now—he is dad's helper. Do not give the baby too much attention in the presence of the younger child. Already, he feels supplanted. With care and consideration parents can do much to avoid and alleviate the upsetting emotion of jealousy.

We have considered a few problems that may face parents of young children. Several others will be discussed in the next chapter.

CHAPTER FIVE

Living Is Learning—With Young Children (II)

. . . To seek of him a right way for us,
and for our little ones . . .
(*Ezra 8:21*).

There is a right way for us and our little ones, a way of understanding and peace. We can learn that right way by seeking wisdom from God, the all-righteous One. The right way involves the Christian approach to problems. Some were discussed in the last chapter. Others are presented here.

Fear

Perhaps the most prevalent problem of the young child is fear—that phobia of childhood. Psychologists tell us that the baby comes into this world with only two fears, the fear of loud noises and the fear of falling. All others are acquired. Now fear in the sense of prudence is necessary. It serves the purpose of race preservation. Such fear makes one cautious and careful. The young child must be taught to be cautious of some things: the fire, strange animals, daring adventures, etc.

Abnormal fear in a little child's life is a terrible thing. The seriousness of childhood fears lies in the aftereffects. They sometimes carry over into later years. Children are sensitive to a degree almost incomprehensible to adults. They may suffer acutely from fears of which the adult has no knowledge.

Parents should try to view fear as the child views it; never ridicule him for being afraid. It is very real to him.

"The fears of children are foolish and unreasonable to us simply because of our limitations in understanding the experiences through which the child is passing or has passed. . . . Few parents take the fears expressed by children seriously enough. . . . There is no emotion to which the child is more frequently subjected than that of fear. It . . . plays such an important part in the development of the personality of the child that it needs most careful consideration." [1]

During infancy fear has a basis in fact. Something happens to the baby to make him afraid. As he grows into early childhood he is beset with imaginary fears. "As he grows older . . . a large number of his fears pertain to distant dangers, forebodings as to what the future may bring." [2] Sometimes we fail to recognize the little child's fear because he is afraid of being considered cowardly and disguises it.

Darkness holds terrors for some little children. As one little girl expressed it, "The dark swallows all the pretty things." The child has little sense of perspective where his fears are concerned. Everything appears big to the small child.

Five-year-old Betty was a shy little girl. She was afraid of the dark and wanted her mother to leave the light on in the bathroom or the hall. Her mother tried to talk her out of it but was unable to do so. She told her mother, "The dark gets into my face." Betty liked to stay near her mother.

Many times the source of fear is unknown. It may be that the child has heard horrible tales from some older child or from the radio. He may have seen some unearthly picture at the movie or on television. Thoughtful parents will avoid such senseless strain on their children.

Fear of the dark may have its source in a guilty conscience. A young child may have hatred in his heart and wish that he could hurt someone. He knows this is wrong and, although he never expresses that hatred in deeds, he fears punishment. Such fears cause dreams and nightmares.

Going to bed at night should be a quiet, unhurried affair. A few moments of quiet companionship after the lights are out have definite value. The fearful child needs to know that he is loved; ". . . perfect love casteth out fear . . ." (I John 4:18). Show him special love. Talk things out with him. One mother spoke of darkness as a blanket covering the earth at night, when the birds, the flowers, and the little animals of the woods were asleep in their beds. Use stories and books to alleviate his fears. One mother found Margaret Wise Brown's book *Night and Day* helpful. This is a story about two cats; one of them preferred the day, the other preferred the night.

It will do no harm to let him have a baseboard light at night. One parent allowed his five-year-old to keep a flashlight under his pillow. He may not use it but it is a comfort to know it is there. It is all right to leave his door open for awhile. He will outgrow the need for it.

Teach the little child that God watches over him during the night just as He does during the day. Many children have found great comfort in the words of David, "What time I am afraid, I will trust in thee" (Psalm 56:3). Five-year-old Elizabeth explained the verse this way: "Sometimes when I go to bed, I think I'm going to be scared. Then I remember about God keepin' care o' me and I'm not afraid any more." Who can say she did not experience that Bible verse? Darkness seemed to hold no fears for her.

A timid child may be afraid of people and of the ordinary experiences of everyday life. Fathers many times make the mistake of insisting that the timid child take his chances along with the rest, while mothers go to the other extreme of protecting and excusing the child to such an extent that he is never required to face his problems or to learn how to take hardship.

The timid and fearful child should have opportunities to meet strangers under favorable conditions. He should not be forced into a new group. He should be allowed to sit by and watch for awhile. Teach him skill in some activity, then encourage him to join the group where he can use that skill.

Change—moving from place to place—also upsets the young child. During the war years many fathers were called out of the home and children traveled over the country trying to keep up with them. Eugene had seen his father go away as a chaplain in the service of his country. He seemed disturbed and moody for some time. One day he burst out with the statement, "Mother, you don't love me any more; you haven't loved me since Daddy went away!"

Children can be spared much of the anguish of leaving the old home for a new one if they are prepared for the experience before it occurs. Parents can discuss the move with them; they can anticipate its advantage. Children can help in the packing. One mother, moving frequently during the war, allowed her two children to pack their own possessions for shipment. Also, each child was allowed one small piece of luggage for his materials to be used for creative activities on the long train trips. Fear of change can be converted into anticipation of new experiences.

Most fears are an outgrowth of the child's home life. Anxious parents, harassed by financial worries or health problems, may pass on to their child a state of anxiety. The young child catches fears from adults. Vague fears of the future may be caused by frequent references to misfortunes that may come. Children, from their earliest years, should be taught to meet and overcome whatever situations may arise. Problems that can be solved by the entire family should be discussed with the children. Problems that cannot be understood by the young child should not be discussed in his hearing.

When one discovers the cause of fear he is on the way to eliminating it. An accurate diagnosis is necessary to wise and efficient treatment. Teaching the Christian concept of God and His care dispels fear in the lives of young children.

Study the child's behavior. Dig under and find the reason for the fear. When the underlying causes have been discovered they should be removed or modified. The greatest measure to offset fear is a faith in a Loving God made real to the child through the parents' daily living. The Christian home should be a happy home and should not harbor fears. Love, happiness, security, and honesty in the home will eliminate most fears. There is a challenge here for parents today so to guide the lives of their children that they may develop a sense of inner peace and tranquility in the midst of world unrest and uncertainty.

Obedience

Learning to obey is another everyday problem for the young child. Since the days of Adam and Eve in the Garden of Eden, obedience has been a determining factor in the religious development of the individual. Of the ten commandments, the only one with a promise is, "Honour thy father and thy mother: that thy days may be long upon the land which the Lord thy God giveth thee" (Exodus 20:12). To honor parents is to obey them. In Colossians we find "Children, obey your parents in all things . . ." (Colossians 3:20).

Early training for obedience is most important. The young child who is taught obedience in the home will find it easier to obey the rules of school and later the laws of the land. Learning to obey is essential to the child's happiness as well as to his future usefulness.

Obedience is not an end in itself; it is a means to an end—self-discipline. Obedience is not for the purpose of breaking a child's will, but for training his will—so that he chooses the right course of action. It is for the child's own well-being. The story is told of two three-year-old boys who went to the hospital with scarlet fever. Johnnie came from a home where he had been taught obedience. Jimmie's parents were too permissive and had never taught their son to obey. Johnnie cooperated with the doctor and nurses. There were uneasy days and weeks but he gradually recovered. Today he is a strong, useful man. Jimmie refused all medicine and food. Day after day, he became increasingly difficult. The doctor, the nurses, and the parents had no control over him. Jimmie became hysterical. Finally, the disease took its toll. Jimmie never recovered.

Parents should strive for an attitude of cooperation. The best type of obedience is that which is not forced. Obedience becomes a means of religious development when the adult appeals to the child's intelligence and obtains his will. Parents should work *with* the child to help him grow in self-control rather than *over* him or against him to force their will upon him.

However, obedience should lead the child to do some things he would rather not do. This training in doing things from a sense of duty must begin in the early years if there is to be self-control in later years. In the beginning this control must be exercised by the parents, for the child. Parents must see that the child does the thing that is best for him, even when he does not want to.

The child must have confidence in his parents if he is to obey them. He must believe that they love him and wish only his good. In order to maintain this confidence parents must be consistent in what they expect of their children. They must be consistent not only in their requests of the child but also in their Christian living.

Sometimes children fail to obey because parents give contradictory commands. Five-year-old Michael's parents did not agree on what they expected of their son. "Mike" refused to eat a balanced diet. He loved milk and his father said, "No child of mine will go without milk as long as I can buy it!" He insisted that his wife allow Mike to drink all the milk he wanted. Mike did! Quarts of it every day! Naturally, Mike was not hungry when he came to the table. The father blamed the mother for Mike's failure to eat. However, when the mother prepared a good meal and Mike "turned up his nose at it" the father allowed the son to "get away with it." He said, "I had to eat things I didn't like when I was a child. You'll just have to find something for Mike that he likes." Mike became a monarch and enjoyed his authority over his parents. For him disobedience brought satisfaction.

Parents should be reasonable. Little children come to accept parental authority when parents are reasonable and just. When children are dealt with understandingly from early childhood they usually develop in self-control and in obedience to those in authority.

Building a happy relationship with your child encourages obedience. If your child respects you and desires your approval he will want to obey. Give him freedom in nonessentials. Prohibit only that which is necessary for the child's best welfare and that of his associates.

Sometimes children do not obey because the request is not made clear to them. Secure your child's attention before you make your request. This usually can be done by calling his name. Then be sure that he understands what you expect of him. Make no more than one request at a time and make it simply and clearly. Too many directions confuse the young child. Use a low, cheerful, expectant tone of voice.

A child's obedience should bring satisfaction when possible. Always there is the satisfaction of unbroken fellowship with his parents. If the request is cheerfully carried out, the *work* should be praised, and not the child. Praising the child can lead to a "better-than-thou" attitude. Commending his conduct encourages its repetition.

If parents are to lead the young child to obey, they must ever cause him to be sure of their love. This requires that parents show justice, mercy, and patience. Remember the aim of obedience is to so guide the child that he will attain self-control.

Truthfulness and Honesty

Truthfulness is one of the fundamental virtues. This virtue involves another commandment, "Thou shalt not bear false witness . . ." (Exodus 20:16). So important is it to the religious development of the child that the meaning of truth and honesty should be taught early.

Sometimes an imaginary story is mistaken for an untruth. To some children, their world of fancy is as real as the world of fact in which they actually live. Children live in a make-believe world and their imaginary stories are a part of that world. It is a mistake to think of them as lies.

Frances Morton gives an account of a four-year-old boy who told his mother he had seen three bears down in the corner of the yard. Said he, "We walked together and then the bears walked away into the woods to find their house!" The understanding mother remembered how a recent visitor had vividly told the story of "The Three Bears." She took time to go with her son, looking for the three bears and their house. Meanwhile, she explained that it could be that the bears were not real but only make-believe out of the story. The boy seemed surprised not to find the bears. Finally, after thinking it through, he said, "I saw three play-bears and they said play-words but they looked sure-enough and they sounded sure-enough." [3]

Imaginary stories must be handled wisely lest the child's imagination be suppressed, and yet he must be led to make the distinction between fact and fancy. An understanding of why he tells them helps in knowing how to deal with them. He usually tells them to please. Sometimes his "tall tales" are what he wishes were true.

Whereas at first he is free and frank, the young child becomes untruthful through mismanagement. Sometimes parents are responsible for young children telling falsehoods—they make them afraid to tell the truth. Even a young child will tell a falsehood if he is afraid that he will be punished or that parents will show disapproval if he tells the truth. He is defending his ego.

Sometimes the punishment is all out of proportion to the misbehavior. Parents should remember the purpose of punishment—to avoid a repetition of the act. When a deed results in unhappiness and dissatisfaction it will likely not be repeated. Then the penalty will be for the child's good. When this is true, the punishment will be less severe.

Parents should assure the child that as long as he tells the truth there will be good fellowship between them, though punishment must follow wrong-doing. The child should be allowed to explain his conduct. His conduct should be studied to ascertain the reason for it. The more wilful he appears, the more he needs understanding guidance.

Some children misrepresent or exaggerate to gain approval for themselves. There is a hunger for recognition and approval. This should be granted through legitimate channels; the temptation for such untruthfulness being thus removed. Another cause for the child telling an untruth is deceit on the part of parents and other adults. A child cannot hear his adult friends tell "white lies" and not be warped in his idea of truth. The young child gets his first lessons of truthfulness in the home. Parents who keep promises made to their children and who speak the truth before them are teaching by their lives.

Honesty is closely related to truthfulness. If we want the little child to be honest we must be honest with him. Recognize his property rights. Give him a place where his things can be kept and respect his ownership of them.

Sometimes a child will be dishonest in order to get attention. Four-year-old Edith refused to enter into church kindergarten activities and usually sat by herself. One day, while the teacher was busy with other children, she slipped another child's toy into her locker. It was discovered after the children went home. This happened time and time again. Sometimes the toy was taken home. A visit to Edith's home revealed that she came from a cultured family. Her father was about to receive his Ph.D. degree from a large university. At the same time he worked to support his family. Her talented mother did a great deal of entertaining. Both loved their children but had little time for them. Edith wanted someone to notice her. She took things to get attention. Also, parents allow a child to be dishonest when he takes more than his share of their time and attention. A child who is demanding and selfish is learning to be dishonest.

One of the best ways to teach honesty is to help the young child realize that this is God's world. He made it and He made us. God has given us the privilege of using His good gifts.

Even the young child is old enough to learn tithing—not legalistic but cheerful tithing! Out of his love for God, he wants to make a gift to the Father. Show him Jesus' teaching: ". . . these ought ye to have done . . ." (Matthew 23:23). Help him to see that ". . . God loveth a cheerful giver" (II Corinthians 9:7). Learning to be honest with God will help the young child to be honest with others.

Parents have a solemn obligation not only to set a trustworthy example but also to so guide the lives of young children that they will want to tell the truth. By their words, they have the opportunity to help children differentiate between fact and fancy. And by their deeds, they may help them to value truth and honesty in everyday living. Children have to be trained to be honest and truthful.

Questions Concerning the Origin of Life

"Sex and religion are not far removed in any age of life —'Blessed are the pure in heart, for they shall see God'—but in children of younger years . . . the two are almost inseparable." [4]

A distorted view of life obtained in early years can mar the child's religious development for all the future. Most parents admit that sex education is important but many seem to have a feeling of helplessness in the matter. In every phase of the child's life parents have the first opportunity and obligation. They may turn over to others this sacred privilege and thus lose an opportunity for increasing the child's confidence in them. "This, however, can never take the place of the fundamental instruction in the early stages of the child's life which only the parents could give." [5] To evade the issue is an injustice to the child.

When parents avoid their responsibility in this matter, they do not keep children ignorant of the facts of life; children seek their information elsewhere. The choice is between half-truth gained from the wrong source, or correct and satisfying knowledge, given with high ideals.

Parents' attitude toward their role in life is of paramount importance here. In a home where parents are considerate and loving toward each other, this atmosphere will be reflected in the personality of their children. A happy home environment is the best insurance for a healthy attitude toward sex. This attitude begins in the earliest years of life.

The mother who is happy in her home with her children is likely to have a daughter who will look forward to motherhood. Likewise the father who gives time and thought to his children can help his son grow up with the feeling that being a dad is a rewarding experience.

Fortunate is the little girl whose father gives her attention showing that he is glad he has a daughter. Happy is the little boy whose father takes him on an occasional fishing trip or excursion and makes him a part of his man's world.

The time to give information concerning the facts of life is when the child first asks a question. Give only the information asked for at the time. When he is ready for more he will come back with more questions. Curiosity concerning life comes early to some children. Some ask questions as early as the age of three. Elizabeth was three and a half years old when she found a baby calf in the barn. She asked, "Where did the cow get it?" One little three-year-old came up with this question, "Where wuz I before I wuz borned?" Regardless of how young the child is, when he asks questions he is ready for information, provided, of course, it is given in language he can understand.

Information concerning life's origin should be given as naturally as information concerning any other phase of life. Do not go into a detailed explanation; just give the answer simply and briefly, without embarrassment.

He will let you know (by his questions) how much he is ready to accept. Give him direct, honest answers in a matter-of-fact tone of voice. When a four-year-old asks, "Where did I come from?" your answer could be, "You grew inside of Mommy." Teach him that God has provided that babies grow there. That will be enough for the time being. Overinforming tends to confuse and bewilder the young child.

Think of sex as a natural subject about which you can speak calmly and freely. You are qualified to give information to your child. It is not so much *what* you tell him but *how* you tell it—your attitude toward the whole matter. A helpful book you can read to your child is Schweinitz's *Growing Up.*[6] Never use the stork story. Attributing the origin of life to the stork is fallacious and is harmful to the child.

His questions present an opportunity to teach about God, the giver of life, and thus promote his religious development. The young child should be told the truth concerning the facts of life. Correct terminology should be used for different parts of the body. He should be taught that God made men and women for the high privilege of parenthood.

The child should be taught that this information is confidential and should not be passed on to other children. Explaining to him that other mothers want to tell their own children these facts, in most instances, will secure his cooperation. He may be told that this is something just between you two!

When the facts of life are given to the young child as he begins to question, the bond of affection for his parents is strengthened and his concept of the power and goodness of God is enlarged. Life becomes more sacred to him. He comes to think of his body as a gift from God and to realize that his part is to keep that body clean and healthy.

The first prerequisite for teaching the young child the right attitude toward the facts of life is a happy home in which parents love each other. Correct teaching in this realm leads to high moral standards. Such standards are involved in the religious development of the child. If we are to help our little children reach their highest and best, "we must help them to develop a reverence toward the human body, toward the creating of life, and toward life itself." [7]

The Problem of Death

Religious leaders of an earlier day stressed the subject of death with the purpose of preparing little children for the experience. Today, we believe that preparation for life is far more important and the subject of death is given less attention. Nevertheless, most young children meet with the experience of sorrow or death in one form or another and begin to ask questions. This problem has a direct bearing on their religious development. Answers to their questions concerning death may influence their entire philosophy of life. It is most important that they be given Christian answers to this profound problem.

Even a baby is affected by the death of a loved one. Paul was very fond of his father. Each afternoon he sat in his high chair near the window watching for his daddy. His father's home-coming was a big event. Paul was not quite a year old when his father was killed in a train accident. For several weeks after that the little fellow would go to the window and chatter away, just as if to say, "Daddy, why don't you come home from work?" After many months, when the minister visited in his home, he went running to him, climbed up into his arms, and rubbed the minister's face with his little hands. His grandmother said he used to rub his daddy's face the same way.

Many times we do not realize that children are faced with thoughts of death. Perhaps it is our own sense of inadequacy that causes us to evade the issue with them. We are quick to recognize the needs of adults. Parents who have sorrow are helped by friends, visits from loved ones, letters, and other expressions. Many times, the sorrow of the young child is overlooked. He finds himself in a new aloneness without knowing how to fill the vacancy. When faced with death the little child is silent. He does not know how to express his feelings.

The death of a pet may be the little child's first experience with real sorrow. Eugene had a beautiful white rat. He made a house for him and placed him in the basement near the furnace. That was the first place he went each day. One morning, just after he had gone down to the basement, his mother heard a cry. When she arrived on the scene, Eugene put his head on her shoulder and wept bitterly. His little pet was dead!

Some children do not express in words their concern over death. They may ask questions about everything else but when they face death they seem to withdraw into a silent concern. Their feelings are too deep for expression. These children need to be drawn out and taken into a confidence that will dissolve their fear and silence. They require gentle dealing.

When the young child faces sorrow or death he needs understanding consideration from adults. The atmosphere in the home is most important at this time; there must be a sense of security. Parents' acceptance of death will have much to do with his attitude. Greater love and deeper understanding are needed to guide him through the experience.

For the Christian, death can be explained as a door or entrance into the Heavenly Home. The little child can be told that the loved one has gone to live in that home, where he will be with God. The words of Jesus mean much: "Let not your heart be troubled. . . . In my Father's house are many mansions. . . . I go to prepare a place for you. And if I go and prepare a place for you, I will come again, and receive you unto myself; that where I am, there ye may be also" (John 14:1-3). Christian parents realize that the Bible has much to offer the young child in the time of sorrow. He can be led to feel the love and care of the Father in a special way. He readily accepts the promises of the Bible.

The child can be told that the body is only a house in which he lives. Just as he sometimes moves from one house to another, yet remains the same child, so some day he will leave this body and move to another home, the Heavenly Home, where there is always joy, love, and peace—a home so beautiful no one has ever found words to describe it fully. This home can be described as a place of perfect happiness, where we will learn more about God and sing praises to Him. He can be told of a loving Father God preparing that other home.

Parents can tell the young child that friends will be there. They can say, "You know how you enjoy playing with your friends here. In that home we will have even greater joy, with our friends and with the greatest friend of all, Jesus!"

Opportunities for growth in spiritual concepts come with the experiences of sorrow and death. After her mother had tried to explain the approaching death of an older friend who had been sick for some time, four-year-old Elizabeth said, "Mother, when Mr. Lovewell goes to live at God's house, he won't be sick any more." If wisely guided through these experiences, little children may come to have a deeper understanding of life and the loving care of an all-wise God.

The Question of Santa Claus

Should children be led to believe in Santa Claus? There is much controversy among Christian people over this question. Some parents firmly believe that Santa Claus should be a part of every young child's life. Others fear that telling children about Santa Claus will shake their faith in Jesus. Some children have been confused about Santa Claus. In their minds he supersedes Jesus. When he was asked: "Why do we have Christmas?" four-year-old Jimmie answered, " 'Cause Santa Claus comes."

"There is no harm in Santa Claus if there is no deceit connected with him and if he is kept in his place." [8] In one family the two young children were told that Santa was a "make-believe" person, that their parents played Santa. They saw Santa in the store, however, and believed in him truly. A year or two after they started to school the truth of their parents' explanation dawned upon them and they began to play Santa Claus to their parents. Even in later childhood they took great delight in filling their parents' stockings at Christmas time. These children had the happy experience and memory of Santa Claus without later disillusionment. Santa will do no harm as long as he is a "play-like" person and Jesus is a real person and the real reason for Christmas.

Because he lives in an imaginary world the young child can accept an imaginary Santa Claus without hindering his faith in Jesus, if we make the distinction clear. The child understands the fun of pretending because he "plikes" himself. Santa Claus should never be presented as an historical character.

Jesus' birth should be real to the young child, and the thought of giving should be presented as a way of expressing love and joy in honor of His birthday. Giving to others is one way of saying "thank you" for Jesus. Making gifts for others can be a way of giving gifts to Jesus on His birthday. Our Bible says: ". . . Inasmuch as ye have done it unto one of the least of these my brethren, ye have done it unto me" (Matthew 25:40). The story of Jesus' birth should be presented as truth and should be given the prominent place in the meaning of Christmas. Santa Claus should have only incidental and passing significance and should be presented as a fanciful tale that has grown out of custom.

For little children, taking Santa Claus out of Christmas would be like taking sunshine out of day. Tell them the tale of Santa Claus simply, with a twinkle of the eye, as all good fairy tales should be told.

The fault is not with Santa Claus but with our presentation of him. We treat him too realistically. We labor overtime to prove that he is a fact, when he should be given as fancy. Give the tale at a separate time and place from the true story of Christmas. Let the children know that the legend grew out of a kindly old man's desire to bring happiness to others.

Let the young child enjoy the fanciful tale with you. Just as they come to think of fairy tales as imaginary so they will see that Santa is a mythical character. Then they will remember that you have been honest with them. They have enjoyed the game of make-believe and are not hurt when they come upon the facts "for real." When Santa is presented in this way, he does not make Christmas less sacred and meaningful. As long as we major on the true meaning of Christmas and minor on the Santa Claus legend, we need not fear the consequences.

Begin early to give Christmas spiritual significance. One family began their preparation on the first day of December. On that night, just before the children's bedtime, the father read the Christmas story as found in Matthew 2:1-11 and Luke 2:1-20. The next day, a family council was called. The children helped to decide the family project for that Christmas. There was just one requirement: the project (gifts) must go to those from whom they expected nothing in return. This custom became traditional with this family. The children looked forward to it!

One Christmas the project was gifts for some children of another race, whose parents were unable to do much for them. The gifts were simple, as little children's gifts must be, but a lot of love went into the making of them. The children thought of the experience as sharing. They gave of themselves to others.

Alongside this annual project went plans and preparation for other gifts. As far as possible the children made their gifts for friends and loved ones. Sometimes it was a gift of candy or cookies. At other times it was only a card, decorated by the child.

Long before the day arrived, they bought their Christmas tree. This, too, was an experience of family togetherness. Even the youngest had a voice in its choice. It was an occasion when the tree was set up and the ornaments of former years were brought up from the basement. A favorite ornament was a shiny star that always went on the topmost tip of the tree. Each year, the children added new ornaments.

After the decorations were up, the lights strung, and the wreath hung in the dining room window, came family altar time. With only the lights from the Christmas tree the family knelt and told God "thank you" for sending Jesus into the world.

Continuing through the Christmas season, family altar time centered around the Christmas thought: peace on earth, goodwill toward men. Christmas carols were sung as they gathered around the piano and an atmosphere of

Christmas cheer pervaded the home. Christmas was a spiritual experience for these children.

Lead your child to think more about giving than getting. Even the young child is not too young to learn ". . . It is more blessed to give than to receive" (Acts 20:35). Encourage him to make some of his gifts. Let him choose the ones he wants to buy.

Avoid overstimulation as the Christmas season approaches. Shield your children from commercial pressure. Make it a time of unhurried, warm experiences. Make Christmas a family festival with Christ at the center. That is why we have Christmas! Plan your activities so that all your time is not taken with doing things *for* your child but rather doing things *with* him. All of us need to play at being Santa Claus. Young children can know the joy of Santa Claus and at the same time can grow spiritually as they are led in unselfish, loving service to others in honor of the birthday of Jesus.

Some of the problems of the young child, directly related to his religious growth, have been presented. We have tried to say that all of life is related to the young child's religious development and that God is interested in everything the child does and thinks and says.

Obviously other problems could have been studied. We hope we have stimulated your thinking so that you will seek further aid.

Remember this, no perplexity the child faces is beyond the realm of God's care. Parents can lead the child, with his anxieties, to our Father God. The Christian religion offers a way of life and a solution to life's problems for every individual, regardless of age.

CHAPTER SIX

What to Teach

. . . Now set your mind and heart to
seek the Lord your God
(I Chronicles 22:19, RSV*).*

"I know that there is a God! No human being could make a personality like this, and it certainly couldn't just happen!" These were words of a new mother, as she talked with a church visitor about her baby. For the first time a college professor's daughter was voicing her ideas concerning the reality of God. She had been taught that God did not exist or at the most to say, "I don't know."

The coming of a little one changed all this. Her defense of doubt and indifference gave way to seeking after God. Said she, "I want my baby to learn about a God of love."

The question may be asked, "What and how shall I teach?" The answer is, out of your own vital faith in God. You cannot teach what you do not believe. It may be that in the stress and strain of life, your faith has faltered and failed. The birth of your baby has brought you back to the reality of God.

Return to that place of private devotion. Your faith can be renewed and your fellowship with God can become warm and winsome. As you read His word daily, pray this prayer, "Lord, I believe, help thou my unbelief." As you deeply yearn to know Him and the power of His resurrection, He will reveal Himself to you. Hear His invitation: "Come unto me, all ye that labour and are heavy laden, and I will give you rest. Take my yoke upon you, and learn of me; for I am meek and lowly in heart: and ye shall find rest unto your souls. For my yoke is easy, and my burden is light" (Matthew 11:28-30). He has promised, ". . . him that cometh to me I will in no wise cast out" (John 6:37). You can count on that promise!

You must *want* His friendship; He will not force Himself upon you. When you turn to Him and take time to let Him speak to you, how sweet your fellowship will be!

Along with your Bible, read about others who have struggled through to victory. Multitudes have walked this way. Some have written a record of their experiences. They will inspire you and give you courage. Eugenia Price tells of her transformed life in her book "*The Burden Is Light*; Dale Evans Rogers relates her story of the upward journey in *My Spiritual Diary*. Listed at the end of this book are other writers whose lives may bless yours.

Knowing God comes by faith. It is more reasonable to believe than not to believe. There has to be a mind back of this world. Matter must be controlled by mind. That mind is God.

Another evidence of God is the creative power of love. There is the love between husband and wife; between parent and child; between friends. Now love did not just happen. It has its origin somewhere, and that origin is

God. ". . . Love is of God . . . for God is love" (I John 4:7,8). Love is the very source of life.

The coming of a new life brings spiritual yearning to the young parents. They begin to seek for the meaning of life; to search for the source of life. Though we may know the scientific facts of life, the birth of a baby is still a mystery. Our Bible tells us, ". . . God formed man of the dust of the ground, and breathed into his nostrils the breath of life; and man became a living soul" (Genesis 2:7).

Parents participate in the biological process of life but they do not create the germ of life. That remains a mystery—without God. "So God created man in his own image, in the image of God created he him . . ." (Genesis 1:27).

When we take time for fellowship with God we find renewal of faith. Faith in God gives meaning to life. He has promised, "And ye shall seek me, and find me, when ye shall search for me with all your heart" (Jeremiah 29:13). Let Him speak to your heart through His word, as well as through the experiences of life.

When parents find God for themselves they are prepared to tell their child about Him. They will not seek to make him conform to adult standards but will attempt to help him develop and reach his maximum spiritual growth at his own age level.

The little child must express his thoughts and emotions in the language of a child. He cannot know all the experiences of an adult. The little child's faith is simple and direct but it should grow in depth and meaning as he is led into expanding experiences. Parents who guide little children must decide what they propose to teach. There must be a conscious effort to reach a positive goal. They must set up objectives that determine the course of action.

Dr. Paul Vieth, Yale professor of Christian nurture, defines an objective as "a statement of a result consciously accepted as a desired outcome of a given process."[1] Objectives crystallize thinking and cause us to see what we want to teach our children. According to Dr. J. M. Price, founder of Southwestern School of Religious Education, "The objectives of religious education are determined by the fundamental needs of human life . . . as the Christian religion is set to help meet those needs."[2]

To guide you in your thinking, the following objectives are set forth: (1) the discovery of God; (2) an understanding and appreciation of Jesus; (3) an expanding love for others; (4) the expression of devotion through prayer and praise; (5) generosity; (6) love of the Bible; (7) love of the church.

The Discovery of God

"It is not too much to say that the concept of God . . . is the most vital issue in the world today."[3] All of life is influenced by one's idea of God. "The distinctive thing in Christian education is God-consciousness, and the experience of fellowship with Him."[4] The correct impression of God is the most important concept a child can have. Because of its importance, the child's idea of God receives first place in a study of religious objectives.

ERRONEOUS IDEAS

Too often children acquire erroneous ideas of God. They surprise us at times. John was a little boy of four. One day he was talking with his mother about his daddy's having to shave. Said he, "When I get big like daddy, I'm not going to shave. I'm going to grow long whiskers like God." This idea of God with whiskers seems to be rather common among children. It may be the result of an attempt to teach the child abstract truths for which he has no understanding.

Some children think of God as a policeman, waiting to punish them when they do wrong. One mother said, "God won't love you, if you do that." One little child thought of God as an old man with a big eye in the middle of his forehead, sitting up in the sky watching to catch people when they do wrong. Never should we use God as a club to scare children into doing right! They must know that God loves them all the time but that it pleases God when they do that which is right.

To four-year-old Jan, God is someone she likes "who lives at church and in heaven." "God has moved to heaven and is there now," said four-year-old Vernon. Five-year-old Rosemary thinks God is up in the sky. Said she, "Jesus flyed up to the sky, too." Three-year-old Johnny asked his mother what God looked like. "I really don't know," she answered. "Well! didn't you see Him when He put your eyes in?" was Johnny's amazed reply.

Four-year-old Leroy attended worship service with his parents. The preacher's text was Isaiah 66:1: "Thus saith the Lord, The heaven is my throne, and the earth is my footstool: where is the house that ye build unto me?" Next day his mother heard Leroy say to his playmate, "Tom, did you know God sits up in the sky and puts his feet on the earth?" "Wow!" Tom answered, "God must have mighty long legs!"

Because religious teachings are imbedded in our culture, all children are influenced by religious beliefs, whether or not they are taught in the home or in the church. Sometimes they get wrong ideas. Mistaken ideas about God may come from church hymns children hear in congregational singing. Eva and Neva were identical twins. One Sunday they came running in from church with happy expressions of joy. Said Neva, "O, Mother, guess what they sang today! They sang 'Jesus loves Eva and me!' "

EARLIEST IDEAS

At a very early age little children begin to wonder about God. Debbie was only two years old when she asked, "Where is God?" Their first ideas of God come from parents in the home. In guiding the little child in his discovery of God, parents and teachers must begin with their own experience. They cannot teach what they do not know. As they have learned to believe, so they must teach the child.

Earliest impressions are made by the atmosphere in the home. Long before the baby understands language, he perceives attitudes. It is believed that he can have a feeling of something different (akin to awe) long before he can realize why he feels that way. As the baby hears the Bible read, listens to the prayers of his parents, and witnesses their spirit of reverence, he receives his first impressions for Christian character.

GOD, A LOVING FATHER

Teach your little child to think of God as a loving Father. His ideas about God will be determined largely by impressions received from the love and care of his parents. If parents are affectionate and kind it will not be difficult to teach him about a loving Father God who cares for him. One little three-year-old girl expressed it thus: "*Isn't* it a blessing we've got God? I don't know *what* we'd do without Him, do you?" [5] This dependent, trustful attitude toward parents and other adults can lead to a trust in the Fatherhood of God.

GOD THE CREATOR

"In the beginning God created the heaven and the earth" (Genesis 1:1). Nature provides one of the best opportunities to teach about God. The beautiful flower, the song of the bird, the cloud floating in the sky, all remind the little child that "He hath made every thing beautiful in his time . . ." (Ecclesiastes 3:11). The little one comes to think of God as the One ". . . who created all things . . ." (Ephesians 3:9), and who orders their existence. He feels secure in this all-wise Providence. Mrs. H. A. Deckert tells of an experience a city child had in seeing God through nature.[6] The little lad had been watching a bird in her nest for days. One day mother and daddy were invited to "come and see"—the baby birds had arrived. The mother bird was feeding her young. Together, they talked about God's care for the little bird friends. The child's mother quietly and reverently said, "He careth for you." That evening at bedtime story hour, they found the verse in the Bible book.

EXPERIENCING GOD

Telling children *about* God is not enough, they must experience Him. Relate God to their experiences of joy and they will want to thank Him. When sadness or disappointment comes, help them to find comfort from the thought that God knows and cares. Help them to think of God as near, not far away somewhere in the sky. "Thou art near, O Lord . . ." (Psalm 119:151). Help them to think of Him as One who sympathizes when they are sad and rejoices when they are glad. God's love reaches them wherever they are.

Elizabeth Harrison illustrates this truth with a story from her kindergarten. John loved his teacher so much that he always wanted to be near her. One day a new child entered kindergarten. Mary Helen was a timid little girl. When the circle time came, Miss Harrison suggested that John allow Mary Helen to sit next to her and that he sit across the circle. "No," said John, "I love you so much I want to be near you!" Miss Harrison inquired, "Can't your love for me stretch across the room?" Finally, John consented. After a little while he raised his hand and said, "Miss Harrison, it stretches!"

Make God a part of *every* day not just Sunday. Help your little child to think of Him throughout the day, not just at the end of the day. The Christian religion is a way of life.

Through experience they must learn that although God loves and cares for His children, He expects them to help with His work. They can help by growing strong bodies as they establish good habits. They can help to make the world beautiful by planting flowers, watering, and weeding them.

Children's experiences must be within the scope of their understanding. Parents and teachers must lead little children to know Him not only in thought but also in experience. Such an experience was expressed by a four-year-old girl who was talking to her teacher. With face alight, she exclaimed, "I think to myself and I say to my mother, 'I wish I could see God!' " [7]

PLEASING GOD

Right living should be the aim as the child grows in his knowledge of God. Help the little child to choose the right because he wants to please God. The result of any teaching about God is measured by the little one's daily life. The little child can be led to love God and want to do that which pleases Him. His idea of God, simple in its early beginning, will expand with his religious development. It should be of deepest concern that the child's conception of God influence his everyday living, and result in his ". . . doing the will of God from the heart" (Ephesians 6:6).

An Understanding and Appreciation of Jesus

Jesus is the perfect revelation of God. He told His disciples, ". . . he that hath seen me hath seen the Father . . ." (John 14:9). Parents and teachers who would guide the little child in his discovery of God must lead him into an understanding and appreciation of the Son of God. Jesus should be kept central in the religious development of the child. The extent to which parents and teachers are able to make Him real to children is measured by their own love and devotion to Him. Attitudes are most important in the realm of religious teaching. "From the earliest days in the home and on through childhood, we may help our children to experience God through Jesus Christ."[8]

If children are to have correct concepts of Jesus these must be given in the home, with the Bible as a guide. Five-year-old Michael's parents did not give him this teaching. He thinks that Jesus had a wife named Mary. Once, someone read a Christmas storybook to him. This was Michael's version of the book: "Jesus decided to become a little baby and God decided to become a father so God took his wife and put her on a donkey and they went on a trip. But they knocked on everyone's door and couldn't find any place to live so they had to live out in the barn with the cows and chickens."

FALSE TEACHING

There must be clear thinking in this matter of presenting Jesus to little children; false teaching here can hinder the child's faith for all the future. The Christian parent should teach that Jesus was human, but that He was more; He was God. Children should be taught that Jesus was a good man, the world's greatest teacher, that He was also God. Either Jesus was God as He said or else He was not a good man but a falsifier. Jesus warned against false teachers when He said, ". . . whoso shall offend one of these little ones which believe in me, it were better for him that a millstone were hanged about his neck, and that he were drowned in the depth of the sea" (Matthew 18:6).

In these early years, children have no difficulty in accepting the stories of Jesus as they are given in the Bible and there is no necessity for considering them "legends." True science has no conflict with true religion. If the child grows up with the idea that Jesus is not only human but also divine, he will accept the miracles of Jesus just as readily as he accepts God as Creator. Neither can be explained but must be accepted by faith—faith that appears to the Christian as reasonable.

Just as one would not explain away the miraculous in telling the stories of Jesus, neither should he emphasize the miracles in such a way that the child comes to think of Jesus as a magician. Rather, the kindness of Jesus and His concern for others should be stressed. Jesus could do these things because He is God's son.

Jesus is more than a great man who can become the children's hero; He is a way of salvation. As the little child grows older and becomes conscious of his need of salvation, Jesus can become his Saviour and Lord. When children have this early Christian nurture, they are more likely to realize their need of a Saviour at an early age.

There should be no misunderstanding at this point. It is not assumed that Christian nurture, outside the work of the Holy Spirit, can ever "grow" a Christian life. It is not agreed that if the child is properly nurtured and brought up in a Christian environment from the days of infancy, he will never know sin and will have no need of a saving experience of grace. To every life there must come a turning point. With the child whose life has been surrounded by Christian influences from infancy, this turning may be a gradual process, but there must come a time of wilful choice. Jesus is the only Saviour this world will ever know.

Parents and religious leaders place their work of religious education of the little child on a solid foundation when they realize that: "Neither is there salvation in any other: for there is none other name under heaven given among men, whereby we must be saved" (Acts 4:12). "There is no way provided by man to stop the terrible growth of sin, to stop the development of all our inborn instincts and powers, and to stop the awful results of sin. There is only one way. . . . Reject the Way and we are lost, eternally lost." [9]

JESUS' BIRTH AND CHILDHOOD

Children should be told of the birth of Jesus. They are interested in His coming as a little baby. Beautiful and impressive are the stories of His birth found in Matthew and Luke. These appeal to little children.

Though the accounts of His childhood are few, there are enough to give children the thought that "Jesus increased in wisdom and stature, and in favour with God and man" (Luke 2:52). It should be the aim of teachers and parents to help children appreciate the fact that Jesus was once a child, that He loved His earthly parents even as children today love theirs, that He obeyed His parents, and that He helped His parents even as children today can help.

THE KINDNESS OF JESUS

Jesus went about doing good. Perhaps the strongest appeal to children can be made by telling them how Jesus helped people. As they listen to the stories of Jesus' kindness and care for people, they are constrained to love Him. Present Jesus as a strong, manly character who chose to give His life in service for others.

When the little child learns how Jesus let others help Him in His ministry to the needy—as the lad with his lunch—he is eager to do things that help others. When you have led the little child to feel a love for Jesus, guide him into an expression of that love—help him to do something for someone else—because he loves Jesus.

JESUS, A LIVING FRIEND OF CHILDREN

Care must be exercised lest children think of Jesus merely as One who lived in the past. The objective should be to make Him so real they will think of Him as a living Friend today. Always, Jesus had time for the children. When the disciples wanted to send the children away Jesus rebuked them with the words, "Suffer little children, and forbid them not, to come unto me: for of such is the kingdom of heaven" (Matthew 19:14). Relate the stories of Jesus to the little child's everyday experiences. He can be led to love this unseen Friend who is always near. It should not be difficult for him to think of this Friend as a daily companion.

One day his mother gave five-year-old Kerry an old billfold. Several hours later she saw him sitting in his father's big chair with a rapt expression on his face. As she drew near she saw her son open the billfold and heard him say, "Hello, Jesus!" In the picture compartment of the billfold Kerry had placed a picture of Jesus, cut from an old Sunday School quarterly. Jesus was real to him.

As the revelation of Jesus grows with the years, the thought of him as a Friend becomes dearer. Robbie Trent tells of a questionnaire that was sent to churches in eighteen states, asking for lists of ten favorite hymns. The song that ranked first was "What a Friend We Have in Jesus." [10]

Jesus is the best revelation of God that this world will ever know. We must tell little children of His birth, His childhood, and how He went about doing good; we must lead them to see that He is a living Friend. This understanding and appreciation of Jesus will come not only from the stories that are told to the children but also from the reality of Jesus' presence in the lives of their parents and teachers.

An Expanding Love for Others

The acid test of the child's religious training is his conduct toward others. If parents and teachers have led him to ". . . walk in love . . ." (Ephesians 5:2), they have reached a high objective. When children are directed in an expanding love for others they develop an attitude that will make for unselfish, courteous conduct toward other people.

LOVE FOR THOSE IN THE HOME

The little child should think of the home as a place God has provided for the family. Father and mother should be thought of as best friends who care for him. He should be led to feel that he can be a helper in that home, where each member lovingly shares in the work and in service for other members of the family. Elizabeth was only three years old when she asked to help "mommy." Although she had to stand on a box she was allowed to dry dishes. Habits of helpfulness and doing one's share can be fixed early in life.

Patterns of conduct for the little child are copied from older members of the family. When mother and father, older brother and sister are thoughtful and considerate, it is to be expected that the preschool child will be loving and kind. When right is done gladly it is made attractive to the child.

LOVE FOR HELPERS IN THE COMMUNITY

In every communuity there are people who make life happier by their services. Even in rural areas, where farmers are relatively independent, there are some helpers to whom the people are indebted. Little children should learn about these workmen. There are friends who provide food: the farmer, the milkman, the grocery man, and others. There are friends who keep people well: the doctor, the nurse, and the druggist. Children should feel a spirit of gratitude toward these for the contributions they make to worthwhile living. This neighborly spirit should result in courtesy and kindly deeds for these helpers. Teach children that all honest work is worthy and is essential to human welfare. Teach them that God approves all labor as long as it helps others.

LOVE FOR PLAYMATES

The little child should learn to play happily with his contemporaries. "Even a child is known by his doings" (Proverbs 20:11). Parents and teachers must know that "no small part of a truly religious life depends on the right *attitude* toward living . . . on comradeship and responsiveness, on wealth of affection and good will." [11] It is expected that the little child shall begin to learn self-control and consideration for others.

Learning to share is one of the aims for this age. Children learn to cooperate through guided experiences in a group. The child who always wants to be the leader must be taught to follow as well. He must discover that domineering and overaggressiveness do not bring satisfaction.

As he experiences the joy of "working together" his love for playmates will grow.

"A friend loveth at all times . . ." (Proverbs 17:17). Jesus taught that one shows love for God when he is loving and kind to others. The little child learns through experience that right brings satisfaction and happiness. He should be led to think of the happiness of others. With patient guidance a little child can be led to ". . . do that which is right and good . . ." (Deuteronomy 6:18). This subject is developed more fully in the next chapter under the topic of play.

LOVE FOR OTHER RACES

Children have no race prejudice until it is acquired from older people. They should be taught that "The Lord is good to all . . ." (Psalm 145:9). Jesus drew no national line. He taught that love for one's neighbor should be equal to love for self. He defined neighbor as one who is in need.

". . . Be gentle unto all . . ." (II Timothy 2:24) should apply to the Mexican child, the Negro child, the Chinese, or to any other child. In these early years foundations can be laid for world friendships.

The Expression of Devotion Through Prayer and Praise

PRAYER DEFINED

Prayer is talking with God. The little child prays when he speaks out of his heart to God. In prayer, there is fellowship with an unseen friend. The prayer may be one of praise as expressed by the Psalmist, "I will praise thee, O Lord . . ." (Psalm 9:1). Little children can be led to experiences in which they will "In every thing give thanks . . ." (I Thessalonians 5:18). Experiences of joy cause the child's heart to overflow in praise to God the Father. One little three-year-old bubbled over with this prayer of praise, "Thank you, God, for lettin' me 'luv' people."

Debbie was not quite three years old when she received a necklace from her grandparents. With her parents she was looking at the gift, when she said, "Let's pray together." They bowed their heads and this was Debbie's prayer: "Thank you, God, for grandma and grandpa. Amen." Her prayers are spontaneous—at any time of the day she feels like it—not just at certain times. For Debbie, prayer is talking to God.

Little children are realistic in their prayers. Four-year-old Mary Ann prayed, "Help daddy to be a good student and help mommy so she won't burn the food."

ESSENTIALS FOR HELPING CHILDREN TO PRAY

If the child is to be led to pray he must have become acquainted with the experience through the example of others. Some of the earliest impressions come from the prayer life of parents. The baby sees the parents at prayer; he hears the earnest, joyful voice; he senses the atmosphere. Out of his own prayer experience the parent or teacher guides the child. If we are to teach children to pray we must pray ourselves, we must understand the child's feelings and thoughts, and we must realize what true prayer is.

If, from earliest recollection, the child has the influence of prayer in the home, there will come a day when he will want to pray. A felt desire is an essential for real prayer.

Out of a heart of gratitude the child's first prayer comes. Elizabeth was two years old when she uttered her first prayer. It was a "tank you for mommy, for daddy, and for baby brudder."

Having a definite time and place can help the child to learn to pray. Many parents have used the bedtime hour for prayer time. Talk over the experiences of the day in their relationship to God. Then kneel in prayer. There, in the quiet of the evening, the little child's heart will open in confidence toward God.

ATTITUDE IN PRAYER

Care must be exercised lest the little child acquire the attitude of a beggar. The child should not get the Santa Claus idea of God—that He is One who gives him anything he wants. He must realize that "no" is an answer to prayer, just the same as "yes." When he considers the good of others he will understand that having his own way cannot always be best. One little boy learned this attitude. He prayed for sunshine because they were planning a picnic. When the rain came he said, "I guess God knew that the flowers needed water." [12]

The little child can be led to believe that God wants to give him what he needs, what is best for him. He should come to think of prayer as a time to make his will conform to God's Will, not a time for obtaining special favors.

Right attitude in prayer leads to a spirit of cooperation. The child realizes he has a part in answering his prayer. There must be a conscious effort on his part. Five-year-old Norman expressed it in these words: "When you ask God to do anything for you, you have to do your very hardest yourself, and He does the last little bit you can't manage. If He did it all, it would spoil you." [13]

VALUE OF PRAYER

"It is only through prayer that we can ever come to realize God as the Great Companion of our inner life." [14] Through prayer the little child gains confidence in God. He learns to trust the Father God's care. Through prayer, fear is replaced by a quiet confidence. Day by day, as the little child talks with God the Father, this unseen Friend becomes very real to him.

The value of prayer can be seen in the life of the little child. As his attitude and conduct change for the better we can be sure that prayer is meaningful for him. Prayer not only brings confidence to the child but it also results in right conduct. Through Christian teaching the child comes to know right from wrong and through prayer he gains a desire to do that which pleases God. He must be led to see that he shows his love for God by what he does. He can be led to know that ". . . The Lord is my helper . . ." (Hebrews 13:6) in his effort to do that which is right.

Generosity

"Giving is a very important form of worship, and the foundation for generous habits in later life may be successfully laid at this time." [15] Early in life the child needs to form the habit of generous giving.

GIVING OF SERVICE

Many times little children express their love by gifts of service. There is a real opportunity for religious development at this point. Affectionate children sometimes grow into cold, indifferent boys and girls because adults fail to cultivate that love. Perhaps they are too busy to respond to the little child's simple expression of love in the form of a handful of flowers (they may be weeds!), a mud pie, or a "beautiful" piece of "handwork."

The child should be encouraged to express his love by some small gift of service. Giving of self in service is the greatest gift of all. As one gives of himself to others, his love for others grows. Five-year-old Elizabeth tucked her tired mother into bed one day. Said she, "Now, you stay here and rest. I'll 'keep care' of the house." This she did, sweeping, dusting, and cleaning as best a little girl could.

GIVING ON SPECIAL OCCASIONS

There are many special occasions that offer opportunities to instruct the little child in giving. Perhaps Christmas and birthdays are the most joyous times. The little child should be encouraged to make his gifts, if possible. The value of his crude gift is not in its intrinsic worth but in his experience of outgoing love for others. Christmas came to have a deeper meaning when five-year-old Elizabeth and three-year-old Eugene made candy and cookies for some neighbor children. Birthdays offer happy times of generous giving when children are allowed to enter into the preparations.

GIVING ON SUNDAY

Giving can be made an experience of worship for the little child. Out of gratitude for the fact that God ". . . loved us, and sent his Son . . ." (I John 4:10), little children can be led to bring their gifts to the church house.

They can be taught that they show their love for God by bringing their gifts on Sunday. Always, children should be told how their gifts are used. This explanation should be made in language they can understand. This experience of giving means more to the child if his offering comes from his own money, money he has received as a gift, as a reward for some extra service rendered, or as his allowance.

Bringing gifts of food or clothes for the needy can be a happy experience of sharing for little children. There was an expression of deep satisfaction on four-year-old David's face as he turned his paper bag upside down and watched the apples and oranges roll out on the table. The Beginner children had been asked to bring fruit for an elderly lady who was sick. Truly, ". . . God loveth a cheerful giver" (II Corinthians 9:7).

Love of the Bible

The Bible is a source book of religious instruction. In it can be found poetry, stories of God's dealing with men, and instruction as to right conduct. The Bible "is preeminently a book of religion." [16]

ATTITUDE OF PARENTS AND TEACHERS

The child's first manifestation of love for the Book will be a reflection of his parents' and teachers' attitude toward the Bible. Adults interpret the Bible to children by their daily living. If the Bible has meaning for them, it will have meaning for children. Children should have happy hours with the Bible in association with adults who bring its message to them. "*The Bible is meant to reach children first through the thinking and the living of their par-*

ents."[17] Teachers and parents must believe that "All scripture is given by inspiration of God" (II Timothy 3:16) if they are to "rightly divide the word of truth" to little children. They must use the Bible as a guide in their own lives and in the lives of children. "The earlier a child sees the Bible used, the earlier will begin his love for the Bible." [18]

Ronald is five years old, a minister's son. He likes to carry his New Testament to church, just as his daddy carries his Bible. He wants his father to mark in his Bible "where he is going to preach." He never fails to say, "Daddy, I enjoyed your sermon." When his father asks, "What did I preach about?" Ronald replies, "God."

A SPECIAL BOOK

If children are to love the Bible they must be led to think of it as a special book that tells about God and about Jesus. There is an old Scottish custom that nothing shall be placed on top of the Bible. Perhaps this is a helpful teaching. The child does need to respect and care for his Bible as he would no other book. He should be led to think of it as God's Word speaking to him that he might know how to please Him. The Bible speaks to hearts and minds and molds character. When a love for the Bible is cultivated in early childhood, it can be a guide for all of life. The value of the Bible in the religious development of the child is considered further in the following chapter.

Love of the Church

Happy is the child in whose mind Sunday is associated with the church. Perhaps it is not too much to say that Sunday has no true meaning for the child unless it is associated with the church. The two are intertwined. The church is a special place just as Sunday is a special day. The objective in the religious development of the child should be to lead him into a joyful anticipation of going to church on Sunday. The little child can be led to say truthfully, "I was glad when they said unto me, Let us go into the house of the Lord" (Psalm 122:1).

SUNDAY IN THE HOME

One of the happiest memories of many adults is that of Sunday in the Christian home. One woman remembers how her mother always put a chicken in the "fireless cooker" on Saturday and baked a six-layer cake. The children pressed the clothes and the father shined the shoes—all in preparation for the Lord's day. When evening time came on Saturday, in one home, the family gathered for the study of the Sunday school lesson.

Even before the baby can be given formal teaching as to the meaning of Sunday, he can be impressed with the fact that it is different. The quiet, unhurried pace of the home, with its spirit of joyful reverence can lead to a feeling that this is a holy day. By careful planning, so that Sunday will be a happy day, parents can give to the child, "the Lord's day to look back upon as his brightest memory, and to look forward to as his fondest anticipation." [19]

It should be the purpose of parents and teachers to give the child a clearer and deeper realization of God's love and God's way on the day that commemorates the Lord's resurrection. True reverence for the Lord's day is shown in gladness; not in gloom and sadness. Elizabeth and Eugene would ask all during the week, "Mommy, is today

Sunday?" Two-year-old Bonnie asks every day, "Is today Sunday Day?" She loves her nursery department and tries to tell the stories when she gets home.

Parents can lead children to find delight in the Lord's day. Jesus sanctioned the doing of friendly, helpful things on the Lord's day when he said, ". . . The sabbath was made for man, and not man for the sabbath" (Mark 2:27). Children will love Sunday when parents make it a happy day. One mother provided a Sunday chest where she collected pictures for the children to cut out and make into scrapbooks for other children. In every way, Christian parents will endeavor to help little children "Remember the sabbath day, to keep it holy" (Exodus 20:8).

SUNDAY IN THE CHURCH

The Lord's day is for the religious development of the individual. Some of this spiritual growth takes place in the church. The church can supplement and enlarge the religious training begun in the Christian home.

The attitude of parents toward the church is reflected in the child. When parents show an interest, his church activities are more meaningful to the child. When he is *taken* to the church rather than *sent* by parents, the child continues to think of the church as a place of importance. Even the little child senses the difference when it is "our" church and parents enter into its privileges and responsibilities.

The objective is to lead the children to think of the church as a place where they have happy times. Some little children think of Sunday as the best day of the week. This was true of a little Chinese boy. Nearly every day, four-year-old Daniel would say, "Is this Sunday?" He wanted to go to Sunday school.

Little Harold came to Sunday school for the first time in many, many months. He wanted to cling to his father and seemed to be afraid of the teacher and the children.

Harold's father was an alcoholic and had been out of work. He loved his family and when he was sober he provided well. But for many months now he had been drinking heavily and had lost his job.

When little Harold drew back his teacher suggested that Harold's daddy remain in the Beginner department with him. The father sat quietly at the edge of the activities. At first Harold took a book to his father to read. Then the teacher told the story to the small group. Harold came to the table and listened. The story was about ten lepers whom Jesus healed and the one man who returned to tell Jesus "Thank you."

Harold's father dropped his head in deep thought. He listened intently as the children repeated the Bible verse: "O give thanks unto the Lord, for he is good." As little Harold left the Beginner department that Sunday there was a smile on his face, and on the face of his father there seemed to be an expression of quiet resolve. When a church friend whom he highly respected suggested that he could get help for alcoholism, Harold's father sought medical aid.

In the church school children learn to cooperate. Sandra was a golden-haired little girl who came from a broken home. When she first came to the Beginner department she snatched what she wanted when she wanted it. Not many Sundays passed before the teacher was able to tell a difference; Sandra was learning to be polite and kind. Sandra came to love the church. One night, at supper-time, her mother could not find her four-year-old daughter. When a search was made Sandra was found in the "big church house," sitting in the pew beside her "teechur."

One Sunday morning a Beginner superintendent asked, "How many of you are glad for the church? Hold up your hands if you are." A little red-headed boy quickly stretched up both hands because he was so glad for the church!

Sometimes children express their love for the church through dramatic play. Four-year-old Jan was playing mother to her two-year-old sister. "Baby, get your coat on; we're going to church," instructed the little mother, dressed in high-heel slippers and old clothes. Soon you could hear the song, "I love my church, I love my church, and oh, I love this day; When Sunday comes, when Sunday comes, I cannot stay away." [20] Jan was standing beside the "pulpit" leading the singing from a picture book.

Because of God's love, He provided a special day and a special place for worship. Little children can be led to associate the two with happy memories and helpful experiences that broaden and deepen their religious development.

Conclusion

If there is to be religious development in the life of the little child there must be objectives to guide parents and teachers. In this chapter there has been an effort to enumerate these aims or goals. These objectives have been related to the child's attitude toward God and toward other children. Repeatedly, it has been stressed that the child's reaction to these objectives is influenced by his parents and teachers. In the following chapter a fuller study is made of the value of these objectives in the religious development of the child, and methods for reaching them are suggested.

CHAPTER SEVEN

How to Teach

. . . The little ones . . . shalt thou
take unto thyself . . .
(Deuteronomy 20:14)

Within the last half-century rapid progress has been made in teaching the young child. Contributions of psychology have been applied to religious instruction. From the day of the card class, when little children sat on high benches and recited their many Bible verses, to the present church school kindergarten, a long road has been traveled.

We have learned that religious development comes to the young child not so much through memorized material as through experiences where religion is made real. We recognize that there must be outward *expression* if there is to be inward *impression.* Religious truths cannot be fitted "ready made" into some groove of the child's mind and life. There must be many vital experiences through which his spiritual nature may grow. We know that the ultimate test of religious teaching is not whether a child has acquired certain facts but rather the influence that teaching has upon his conduct and attitude toward others.

First of all, let me emphasize again that we teach by what we are. Our own personal lives have the greatest influence upon our little ones. Some say, "spiritual truths are caught rather than taught." John Milton Gregory tells us that "Teaching, in its simplest sense, is the communication of experience." [1]

Nevertheless, there are definite avenues of approach to the soul of the child. Recognizing his characteristics and following his unfolding life, we have opportunities to teach about God. It is an informal teaching woven into the fabric of his everyday life.

Some of these avenues of approach or methods of teaching are through: (1) nature study; (2) the use of the Bible; (3) the use of stories; (4) books; (5) conversation; (6) pictures; (7) music; and (8) through play and creative activities.

Teaching Through Nature Study

Nature-study gives the child a sense of companionship with life out of doors and an abiding love of nature.—Anna Botsford Comstock[2]

Even a baby is affected by the beauties of the out-of-doors. Two-month-old Jean Carole was crying when her mother moved her bassinet to the picture window where she could see the trees. Immediately the crying ceased. For a long time she was content as she gazed out upon the world of nature.

At eight months Jean Carole smiled and clapped her hands when grandmother started her on her "baby-buggy walk." As they went along the tree-shaded street, her little face turned upward with an expression of glowing content. Her eyes followed the flight of the birds, the movement of the leaves, and the pretty flowers. When they stopped to look at—and touch—a beautiful flower, grandmother sang softly: "Oh, who can make a flower? I'm sure I can't, can you? Oh, who can make a flower? No one but God 'tis true." [3]

Jean Carole was getting impressions and developing a love for the out-of-doors. She will learn to associate nature with nature's God. When her unfolding powers permit, her parents will say to her (as she views God's handiwork), "In the beginning God created the heaven and the earth" (Genesis 1:1). They will explain to her the meaning of the word "created" and will find the verse in her Bible, letting her put her finger on it.

Living creatures fascinate the small child. Eugene was only three years old when he came in from the back yard with a caterpillar crawling up his arm. He wanted a "house" for his new discovery. His mother put the caterpillar into a jar and punched a small hole in the lid. Turning to Comstock's *Handbook of Nature Study* they found facts about the creature. Day after day Eugene put food in the jar and observed the changes. One day, he exclaimed, "Oh Mommy, come quick, there's a big fly in my jar!" The caterpillar had emerged into a beautiful moth. Together they found their Bible and read, "He hath made every thing beautiful in his time . . ." (Ecclesiastes 3:11). The oft repeated verse took on new meaning for that three-year-old.

Give your child opportunities to enjoy the out-of-doors. There are lessons to be learned in your own back yard. When he shows interest in the things of nature, talk with him about them in simple language he can understand and relate them to God.

Perhaps you say, "But I live in an apartment in the city." There are the parks, provided for you and your children. One mother, living in New York City, set aside a portion of each afternoon for a visit to the park. That was the only time her two children put their feet on the grass. In the midst of the "hustle and bustle" of that city stands Central Park, inviting mothers to teach their children about nature. For the Christian parent, this offers an opportunity to point to the Creator of nature.

The young child should be taken out-of-doors where he can feel the infinite rhythm of the universe. His questions should be answered just enough to make him want to explore further, not enough to explain away wonder. He should experience the rain, the wind, and the sun. He should be taken into the deep, deep woods. He should hear the bird songs in the spring, and see the rabbit tracks in the winter. In the lazy fall he should have the experience of looking for the goldenrod, the autumn leaves, and the wild flowers of the field. The things of nature are God's gift from His out-of-doors and they can be one of the first avenues of approach to Him.

Especially when it occurs in the out-of-doors, nature study allows children a time for slowing down (a thing much needed in our speeded-up world) and an opportunity for wonder—getting under the surface of things to the *how* and *why*. This results in fleeting moments of awe and reverence, which can be explained by neither the child nor the adult, but which point to God, the Creator.

Down by the seashore, picnicking in the park, camping in the summertime, wherever you go, explore the possibilities of nature study. These out-of-door excursions need to be supplemented by nature objects that are brought indoors. The care of small pets, such as fish, turtles and other creatures, can provide many teaching experiences as well as pleasure for the small child. The flower box, tended by the child himself, will have deeper meaning when it is related to God. Young children can be led through this wonder and awe in the presence of the visible things of nature into a reverence and love for the invisible Creator. "For by him were all things created, that are in heaven, and that are in earth . . ." (Colossians 1:16).

Nature study is sacred ground, for it is here under the guidance of Christian parents and teachers, that God speaks to the hearts of little children. In nature study children find the never-ending satisfaction of discovery as they observe the little creatures of earth and water. Every experience with nature can add to their knowledge of God and to their sense of dependence upon a loving Father God.

Using the Bible to Teach About God

The Bible would be pre-eminently *the* child's book even though it had no religious value above other books.—John Ruskin

The Bible is central in the teaching of the Christian religion. It is our guide. Already, we have pointed out that it is valuable to the young child as we relate it to his every-day life. "For the little child, the Bible portrays God as a loving Heavenly Father, who made the world in which he lives and who watches over him as an unseen Friend." [4]

From the Bible come teachings that relate to all of our objectives.

In the home, the Bible may be given to little children in its entirety. Some parents do just that. As soon as the child is willing to listen the mother begins with the first chapter of Genesis. Of course, this is at a time and place best suited to the child. The mother reads in the child's language. When long lists of names come she skips over them and continues the thread of the story. She studies the Scripture passage ahead of time and is prepared to "translate" it into words that have meaning for her child. When she finds a portion that is not suitable, she leaves it until her child is older and can better understand it. The beautiful passages in Psalms and other parts of the Bible she gives to her child just as they are.

Although the young child may not understand all of the words, the Bible speaks to his heart. One mother tells of an experience in reading the Bible to her little five-year-old girl. She had read about Jesus, from His coming as a babe in Bethlehem to His crucifixion on Golgotha's hill. " 'It is the saddest story we ever read, mother. But I like it best of all,' " the child said. One day, the little daughter asked, " 'What will we do when we have read *all* the Bible, mother?' " When her mother replied that they would read it all over again, and that when baby brother was big enough they would read it again to him, the child added, " 'And we won't ever get tired of it, will we?' " [5]

The principles of the Bible apply to young children as well as to adults. There are those who would leave the teaching of the Bible to later years. They seem to think that the Bible presents too many problems for these early years. We take the position that such problems and questions are largely in the minds of parents and teachers, not in the minds of the children or inherent in the Bible. It is believed that the idea of considering the facts of the Bible as fancies originated with those who refuse to accept the declaration of Paul, ". . . it is in truth, the word of God . . ." (I Thessalonians 2:13).

Parents who have found the Bible a true guide in life's experiences are able to share it with their children. Admittedly, there must be explanations and these will be given in the light of faith, not in the shadow of doubt. Some portions of the Bible may not be suited to the young child. These may be left for later years. Choosing the Scriptures the young child can understand, attempt to make them most meaningful to him.

Experiences with the Bible will be more meaningful to the young child if it is his very own book. His Bible should have large print so that he can more easily read it when he grows older. Pictures in his Bible make it more attractive, too. Give him his Bible at an early age but teach him how to care for it. At first, you will need to handle it for him, placing it on a low table where he can see and touch it. Soon, you will see him turning through its pages, looking at the pictures, just as he does his storybooks.

Throughout the day, relate experiences to the Bible. Use Bible verses naturally as they apply to the child's activities. Help him find the verse in the Bible and allow him to put his finger on it while you talk about its meaning.

Suppose it is a rainy day. There are many Scriptures that teach that God is the giver of rain. Some of these are: Leviticus 26:1-4, Psalm 135:1-7, and Job 5:8-11. Our Bible tells us He "sendeth rain on the just and on the unjust" (Matthew 5:45).

Perhaps it is your first excursion of the year. Warm weather has come. You take a picnic lunch and go into the woods. Here you listen to the singing of the birds, watch the squirrels hopping in the trees, and smell the sweet perfume of wild flowers. This is the time to take your Bible from the car—it is good to keep one there—and read the inspiring words of Psalm 104:10-14, 16, 17.

It was evening time. Five-year-old Shirley was standing by the picture window, gazing up into the sky. She looked at the stars for some time and then she said, "God is turning on the lights up in heaven." Her mother left her supper dishes and together they found the nineteenth chapter of Psalms. Shirley's father joined the group and read to them this majestic chapter from God's Word. This experience made a deep impression upon that little girl.

Do you see what we mean by relating the Bible to life's experiences? With the aid of your concordance you can find a scripture for nearly every occasion.

Teaching the little child to be helpful promotes his religious development as it is related to the Bible verse: ". . . we are helpers" (II Corinthians 1:24). When happy times are followed with the Scripture, "For thou, Lord, hast made me glad . . ." (Psalm 92:4), the young child associates gladness with God.

It must be remembered that a child has not really learned a Bible verse until he has experienced it. When the Bible teaching enters his life and causes a change of attitude we can know that there has been real teaching. Otherwise, there has been rote memory only. Jean and

Jane wanted the same book. Back and forth the book seesawed as both little girls tugged at it. All the while Jean was admonishing Jane: "Be ye kind, be ye kind, be ye kind." Jean had memorized the Bible verse and to her it meant that Jane should be kind to her and let her have what she wanted. The test of our Bible teaching is the conduct of our children.

The Bible can be related to the young child's problems. Already we have suggested Scriptures to use with specific problems. Four-year-old Timothy was having trouble adjusting to others. He could not get along with "friends" who came to play. There was continual quarreling and ill will. One day, when company was expected, Timothy's mother turned to the eighteenth chapter of I Samuel and read the first four verses, adapting the words to the little boy's understanding. Looking at a picture of David and Jonathan, they talked about friends and ways to be friendly. Then they found "A friend loveth at all times . . ." (Proverbs 17:17). Timothy's mother explained that it is easy to love a person when he is "good" but that it takes a *strong* boy to love a friend when he is unlovely.

It may be that your small child is developing a demanding attitude, always getting but never giving. He needs to learn gratitude, to say "thank you" for God's good gifts. The book of Psalms is filled with praise songs. One of the most beautiful is Psalm 136. Read the first nine verses and then skip down to the last two. Repeat the reading. Now you and your child may become a verse choir—of two!—and say it together. You will read the first part of each verse and he can join you on the refrain "for his mercy endures forever." Explain that God's love and kindness lasts always and always. The child will not understand all of the Psalm but he will enjoy the experience with you. He can understand that God is good to give us this beautiful world, with the sun, the moon, and the stars, and to provide food for all His creatures. Through this experience, lead the child to express his own gratitude to God. Help your child to see that he is giving thanks unto the Lord when he says "thank you"—either in word or deed—to loved ones and friends.

Another teaching on the subject of gratitude is found in the story of the ten lepers (Luke 17:11-19). Any problem will need many Scriptures and many experiences. A new positive habit must take the place of the old negative one. First comes a change of attitude. Then, a change of conduct. Encourage the new conduct pattern until it becomes a fixed habit.

Study your child and study your Bible. You will find Scriptures to meet his every need. When a problem confronts you, plan a series of Bible verses to meet that need. Do not hesitate to repeat passages. The young child likes repetition. As you solve his problems you will find a solution for your own.

Using the Bible with the individual child should not take the place of the family altar. Here the Bible has special recognition because it is a family affair. It has the added prestige of father and other members of the family. Your Scripture reading at this time will not be overly long. Let the young child participate in the experience, too. He can arrange the chairs for the family gathering, unless, of course, they are already seated around the breakfast table. He can bring the Bible to the family circle. He can choose a song for the family altar time. Discuss the Scripture selection with the family group. Many periodicals offer a guide for family altar time. One of these is *Home Life*, a Christian family magazine, published by Broadman Press. Introducing the Bible passage for each day is a suggestion for the parent to use with young children.

Whatever guide you follow, try to bring the Scripture reading within the understanding of the young child. Let nothing keep you from the family altar. Keep it regular but informal. Vary your procedure but do not vary your time, unless providentially hindered. Nothing you do with your children will be more meaningful than the family altar.

When the Bible becomes a part of life in these early years, it continues to be vital during all the years. Happy experiences await you and your children as you delve into the Bible truths!

Teaching Through Stories

I would rather be the children's story-teller than the queen's favorite or the king's counselor.—Kate Douglas Wiggin

One of the most pleasant ways of guiding the young child's religious development is by way of the story. The story told has many advantages over the story read. Looking directly into the faces of the children, the storyteller establishes empathy with her listeners and a closer bond is knit. Forever after, she is a dear friend to the children. Freed from the printed page she can make the characters "come alive" for her children.

The story furnishes the mother one of the greatest avenues of approach to the soul of the child, and her first duty to her child is to nourish his spiritual life. One adult, looking back upon his childhood, remarked, "I don't think a home is a home without a story hour."

By means of the story, a mother may gain the confidence of her child to such an extent that a close comradeship through the years will result. The bedtime can become one of the happiest memories of childhood. When the story becomes a part of this quiet-hour, it brings a feeling of contentment and releases influences that can work in the subconscious throughout the night. A story based on a child-life situation, a Bible story, and a prayer time can bring to the children a benediction for time and eternity. No child should be cheated of this evening hour, this happiness and comradeship with his parents.

We are constrained to say, with Partridge, that the home is the great guardian and educator of the individuality of the child. The delightful experience of story-telling should be associated with the home and the family circle.[6]

The Bible is the world's greatest storybook. Within its pages are stories that teach about God. Bible stories can be used to interpret life to the young child. They can aid in establishing attitudes and ideals. Bible stories offer little children "simple conduct patterns of kindness, graciousness and right living; standards that are pleasing both to God and to good people." [7]

Just as the reading of the Scripture and the finding of Bible verses meet the needs of the child, so the Bible story can help him, too. Almost every type of story can be found within its pages.

Bible stories deal with human experiences about which children want to know. That is why they appeal to the interest of even the youngest child. When told to children during the early years, they leave lasting impressions. A young child's faith is simple, and he readily accepts the love and presence of an all-wise God. As he listens to the stories of Jesus, which reveal God to him, he comes to love this unseen Friend. The story form presents the Bible in a way the child can best understand and assimilate. It helps him to see the beauty and joy of right-doing and the ugliness and folly of wrong-doing.[8]

The young child likes stories of babies and other little children. Give him the following familiar stories: Baby Moses (Exodus 1:1—2:10); Baby Jesus (Matthew 1:18—2:12; Luke 2:1-20); Little Boy Samuel (I Samuel 1,2:1-11, 18-20); The Boy David (I Samuel 16:11, 17:14, 34-35; Psalm 23); A Little Jewish Maid (II Kings 5:1-16); The Boy Jesus (Luke 2:40-52); Little Boy Who Gave His Lunch to Jesus (John 6:1-13; Matthew 14:13-21; Mark 6:30-44; Luke 9:10-17); Jesus and Jairus' Daughter (Matthew 9:18-25; Luke 8:41-56); The Boy Timothy (Acts 16:1-3; I Timothy 1:2,18,6:20; II Timothy 1:2,5).

There are Bible stories to fit the seasons. In the spring, tell the Creation story found in the first chapter of Genesis. During the summertime, perhaps on a camping trip, tell the story of Supper in the Summertime found in John 6:1-13, Matthew 14:13-21, Mark 6:30-44, and Luke 9:10-17. For the fall, there is the story of The Big Rain in I Kings 17:1-8, 18:1-2,5, 41-46. To help you understand this story read also Genesis 1:9-10, I Kings 16:30-33, Psalm 147:7-9 and 68:9, Joel 2:23, and Amos 4:7. In the winter tell the story Making Friends in the Wintertime in Acts 27:12—28:11. A story for Valentine's Day could be Good Friends: Jonathan and David. Easter means much to the young child when he is told the Resurrection story in Matthew 28:1-10, Mark 16:1-11, Luke 24:1-34, and John 20:21. An appropriate story for Thanksgiving—A Happy

Day—is found in Nehemiah 12:27-47. Read the entire book to help in your preparation. We have previously mentioned the story for Christmas, Jesus' Birthday.

If you want to develop a love for the Bible, these stories will help: Taking Care of the Bible in Exodus 25:1-2,10-16, 37:1-5, 40:16-21, Deuteronomy 31:24-26; The People Listen to the Bible in Nehemiah 8:1—9:3; Preacher Paul Reads the Bible in Acts 15:22-35; and Philip Shares the Bible in Acts 8:1-6,25-40.

Best of all are the stories of Jesus. Beginning with Jesus as a baby, tell of his boyhood, and then tell of his many helpful deeds. Some of these are: Healing the Centurion's Servant in Matthew 8:5-13, Luke 7:1-10; Stilling the Storm in Matthew 8:18-27; Giving Sight to a Blind Beggar in Mark 10:46-52; Jesus and the Multitude in Matthew 15:29-39, Mark 7:31—8:9; Healing a Little Girl in Matthew 15:21-28, Mark 7:24-30; The Story of the Good Samaritan in Luke 10:25-37; God Cares for You in Luke 12:22-32; Making a Crooked Back Straight in Luke 13:10-17; Jesus and Little Children in Mark 10:13-16, Matthew 19:13-15, Luke 18:15-17; and The Triumphal Entry in Mark 11:1-11, Matthew 21:1-11,14-17, Luke 19:29-44, John 12:12-19.

There are many more stories for the young child. As you read your Bible you will find them. When you do, read the Scripture passage in different translations. Look up unfamiliar words in a Bible dictionary. *Harper's Bible Dictionary* is a good one. Locate the place of the story in a Bible geography. *The Westminster Historical Atlas* will help you.

Study the background of your Bible story. The more you know of its land and people the more real the story will become. Read about them in Miller's *Encyclopedia of*

Bible Life. Because the setting and the customs are so different from our own, Bible stories require more time for preparation.

Visualize the Bible characters. With the aid of your concordance find every Scripture that refers to each. Learn about them from Bible commentaries.

Not only Bible stories but also stories from child life promote the religious development of the young child. Any story that helps to build correct character traits has religious value. Parents should study the technique of storytelling. Some churches offer courses in this art. Many adult education programs include a course in storytelling.

Stories have power to stir the emotions and move the will to right conduct. In an effort to teach kindness to animals the kindergarten teacher told the story of How Spot Found a Home.[9] As the kitten walked down the alley "meowing" because he could find no place to live, five-year-old Joe—whose heart was full of love for everybody and everything—suddenly exclaimed, "Don't say that again! I can't stand it!"

The storyteller who weaves a magic spell with her narrative of familiar things and people, with its repetition of sounds and phrases, fires the child's imagination and challenges him to imitate the beloved character in the story. The good story has an inner spiritual quality.

In every age . . . really great teachers who have had character-building as a conscious aim have known the value of the story and have made it a most effective means of shaping the lives of both old and young.[10] It should be stressed that the purpose in storytelling is not necessarily to impart facts, but to cultivate the emotions in order to arouse the desire to do right.

CHOOSING THE STORY

The story for the youngest child will be more like a one-way conversation. As the parent plays with the baby's fingers and toes, he talks about them. As he dresses the little one, combs his hair, or ties his shoes he "makes up" a running-account story. As soon as the baby learns to focus attention upon a picture he invents a talking-about-it story. As the little one develops mentally and emotionally the stories grow in length and meaning. They should contain many words with sense appeal.

The young child's story must be brief and about familiar things. He enjoys much repetition in his story and he likes to have his stories repeated. He may assist you in the telling of an old familiar tale! By all means, insert some jingle or rhythmic phrase in the narrative. Never mind if it was not there originally, you can make up a rhyme! Have this rhythmic phrase recur as often as feasible. The small child will get a chuckle from it. To him it is like meeting an old familiar friend.

Another thing to look for in stories for this age is animal calls and sounds. There must be continuous action, of course—something doing all the time, not excitable but moving. Too much description is boring to the young child. A simple plot is all that is necessary.

PREPARING AND TELLING THE STORY

A musician would not think of playing for others a number he had not prepared, nor should you attempt to give to others a story you have not prepared. Once you have chosen your story you must make it yours by study. Read it over and over, letting the imagination picture the characters and the incidents. As you go about your work you can think through the story. When the characters of the story "come alive" for you, you can make them live for your listeners.

Then you are ready to analyze the story, selecting its four parts: introduction, body, climax, and conclusion. The introduction or first line should be memorized. Thus you will not be hindered by self-consciousness or loss of your story. The introduction ushers in the characters in the first sentence.

In the body of the story see that the incidents flow along freely, one after the other. This part of the story—as well as the climax—is told in your own words. The climax is the highest point of the story—the part for which all the other is told. Make it stand out—dramatic and full of suspense. The pause can be used effectively here.

After the climax bring your story quickly to a close. The conclusion comes sometimes in just a sentence. One story concluded with "And this is all about him I guess!" It is well to memorize this last line, thus avoiding the tendency to run on and on and on. Resist the temptation to tack on a moral. If the story was well-told your child has already been impressed with the truth and will want to imitate the good. Allow a brief pause at the conclusion to permit the child full enjoyment of the story. Do not break the spell of magic by probing him with questions. If you must question leave that for the recall time.

When you feel that the story has become yours, you are ready to tell it to your child. Sit on a level with him, where you can look into his eyes. Should he become restless, you can touch him and call his name, thus taking him in on the story.

An effective use of the pause can help to hold the attention of the child. Use gestures naturally and sparingly. Keep the voice low and well-modulated. Never attempt to talk above a noise. Give feeling to sense words; make the happy words light and joyful, the sad words low and mournful. Change your voice to suit the different characters. As you visualize the story you will make it real to your child. Your reward will be a deep sigh of satisfaction and the plea, "Tell it again."

Included in the Suggested Reading are books that will help you with the telling of stories. Try it! Remember, your child will think you are the best storyteller ever!

Teaching Through Books

I wonder what families do that don't read books together? It's like not knowing each other's friends.—Annis Duff [11]

Dr. Arbuthnot tells us that books meet many needs of the child. Children have the need for security: material, emotional, and spiritual, which includes: the need to belong—to be a part of a group; the need to love and to be loved, the need to achieve—to do or be something worthy; the need to know; the need for change; and the need for esthetic satisfaction.[12]

Since books do meet the needs of young children, they are the rightful heritage of all. Some of the happiest memories of childhood are associated with books.

From the earliest years, Elizabeth and Eugene had their own books. They were few in number but the best the budget would allow. When their father attended a convention or went away on a trip he brought home a book for each. Christmas and birthdays included an appropriate book. They took great pride in their own books, looking at them again and again. The favorite books became so worn that pages began to fall out and the binding became loose. Four-year-old Elizabeth would "read"—looking at the pictures!—to her younger brother, Eugene.

Their personal library was supplemented by books from the public library. Because of their father's work they moved frequently. At each new home, they obtained a library card. Friday afternoon, when they went to the city library and selected books of their choice, was a great adventure.

Every child should have his own "home library." Each book should be selected with care, to meet the child's specific needs. One of the first books should be a Bible with large, clear print, illustrations in color, and strong binding. The young child will gladly claim it as "my Bible."

Bible storybooks should be included in this library. One that our children enjoyed is *Standard Bible Story Readers*, books One and Two. This is an old favorite that remains popular today. Beautiful pictures illustrate Bible scenes. There are other, more recent ones: *Bible Friends* by Ruth S. Gray; *Jesus, Once a Child* by Sadie Holcombe Davis; *A Star Shone* by Robbie Trent; *Just Like Jesus* by Hattie Bell Allen; *Children of Bible Days* by Florence Hearn, and many others. These are beautifully illustrated and make the Bible very real to the young child.

Mother Goose charms the little child and should have a place in his library. There are many early as well as modern editions. Examine them all and choose the one best suited to your child. Dr. Arbuthnot's discussion[13] can aid you in your decision.

Picture books have a place in the young child's library.

Many times the picture book offers his first experience with literature. The pictures should be about familiar people, things, and facts. It should be of a size that little hands can easily manage. The pages should have a dull surface and be of tough paper. The book should be well-bound and the cover should be of a hard, washable, material. In other words, the young child's picture book should be one that will survive much handling.

Long before he can read, the young child can recall the action of the story by means of the pictures. Therefore the pictures in his book either should tell a continuous story; that is, they should be linked one to the other, or else each picture should tell a complete story. Since pictures supplement actual experience for the little child, they should be clear and accurate. The colors should be bright and the subject matter realistic, familiar, and should portray action. When we speak of bright colors we mean harmonious, pleasing colors, not harsh, noisy ones. The picture should be as large as the book will allow, page size if possible. It should include no more than two or three objects, with little background and detail.

The picture book should be altogether attractive, because it can have esthetic value for the young child. This type of book may cost more than we are accustomed to paying. We need to be reminded that good books are an investment in character and that character is easily influenced at this early age. One of the best ways to build character during these earliest years is by means of the picture book.

There are many lovely books for young children. Go to your public library, to the children's room; the librarian there will guide you along the reading road. Consult the

Horn Book, a magazine that keeps you informed about new books for children and young people. Many happy hours await you and your children!

During these early years it is easy to interest the child in books. At the age of nine months, Jean Carole looked at the pictures while her face registered joy as the lines were read. When her mother was only two years old she "listened" to picture books. Mrs. Duff [14] began reading to her daughter when she was only "half-past one."

Children will be attracted to books when parents have fun with them. Parents take the initiative and soon children begin to choose for themselves. There are many guides to help you in your choice of books for children. Mrs. Duff's own book, *Bequest of Wings,* is an inspiring account of her "family's pleasure with books." It can be an aid to your family. Lillian Hollowell's *A Book of Children's Literature* gives standards by which to choose children's books.

Poetry should have a place in your child's library. *Mother Goose* introduces rhyme. Robert Louis Stevenson's *A Child's Garden of Verses* is an old favorite. A. A. Milne's *When We Were Very Young* is another. Lewis Carroll, Walter de la Mare, Eleanor Farjeon, Eugene Field, Kate Greenaway, Laura E. Richards, Christina G. Rossetti, and many others have written poetry for this age. Some of their poems can be found in Isabel J. Peterson's book, *The First Book of Poetry.*

Begin early to read poetry to your child. Bring out its melody and movement, its "tune and runningness"—Walter de la Mare. Enunciate the words clearly, rounding out the vowel sounds. Read just for pleasure and your child will enjoy it, too. This joy in living provides a splendid environment for your child's spiritual growth.

How do picture books and poetry relate to teaching the child about God? They meet the child's need for security. When the child feels the warmth and security of his own family group, he is receptive to teaching about that larger family—the family of believers—the children of God.

Any book that gives the child pleasure adds to the development of his spiritual life. A happy child is a healthy child, physically, mentally, and spiritually.

Alongside the picture books should go religious books, other than the Bible storybooks. There are many heartwarming books that teach about God and His love.

Robbie Trent has given us a number of such books; they have found wide acceptance among Christian parents. Jessie Orton Jones has contributed to the small child's library of religious books. There are many other authors.

There are books to fit the child's every need. If you want to teach him an appreciation for community helpers read to him Jene Barr's books: *Mr. Mailman, Policeman Paul, Baker Bill,* and others. If you would cultivate a love for children of other races, give him Schneider's book, *Follow the Sunset.* If it is nature study you wish to pursue, there are books to help you there, too. Among others, our children enjoyed *The Bird Book* by Shankland.

No doubt you will be unable to have all these books in your home. Some of them you will not find in your public library. Why not start a church library or if you already have one, add to it books for the young child? Many times the youngest are overlooked; some may not have books in their own homes.

"Books are no substitute for living, but they can add immeasurably to its richness." [15] Many come off the press each year. Choose the best and enjoy them with your children, giving them first of all *the* Book, the Bible.

Teaching Through Conversation

Conversation between parent and child should be a commonplace occurrence, an experience both delightful and profitable. Naturally, it is the adult who must lead the way.—Mary M. Thomson[16]

Conversation with the young child can promote his religious development and afford a delightful experience for his elders. Questions about life can introduce conversations that lead the little child to an attitude of reverence and trust toward God. In the home parents can so guide the conversation of the little child that he discovers spiritual truths. The Psalmist expressed it, ". . . to him that ordereth his conversation aright will I shew the salvation of God" (Psalm 50:23).

In conversation, children reveal their thoughts. Little Eleanor had just heard of the death of her colored nurse, whom she had loved since infancy. " 'You mean God came down last night and got her?' she questioned. Then came her deep thought, 'I was wishing I could see God.' " [17] Children divulge their attitudes and ideas in conversation. These can be clarified or corrected in "talking it over" with adults. Out of conversation with their elders children evolve a philosophy of life that influences all their future years.

Objects and environment can stimulate and guide conversation. Pictures, nature objects, books, and many other things can be used to draw children into conversation. Four-year-old Shirley was talking to her father about a picture she had just "colored." Said she, "This is the church, and here is the office and over there is the organ and on the table is the offering plate." Pointing to a large oval shape in the center of the picture Shirley continued, "There is a church door and these are the people" (pointing to lines in the door).

Activities encourage conversation. As children play at homemaking they carry on conversation with each other and with their dolls. The parent, with a listening ear and understanding heart, can gain much insight here. Block-building provides opportunity for talking together. In fact, conversation can be a chain that links together all the activities of the day. Because children's interest and attention span is brief, conversation will be fleeting and varied.

Children express confidence with their questions, and parents who listen to their children deepen the bond of affection between them. Parents who are "too busy" lose one of life's greatest opportunities. Charlotte repeatedly ran into the kitchen with questions. When her busy mother answered them all with, " 'I don't know,' Charlotte stamped her little foot and said, 'Mommie, you don't know much, do you?' " [18]

In group conversation around the dinner table or in the family circle, children learn courtesy. They learn to take turns in sharing their experiences. They learn to listen while others talk. This sharing period offers an opportunity for every child, even the youngest, to tell of his experiences.

Parents who cultivate a "listening ear," who try to meet

the young child on his own level, can have rich experiences in conversation with him.

Teaching Through Pictures

Pictures are teachers. They tell children stories they cannot read. Pictures speak the language of childhood.—Pauline Hargis[19]

Children love pictures. One has only to watch a young child coming into a room where there is a beautiful new picture and see him drawn to it as if by a magnet to realize that children love pictures. They take pride in having pictures of their own. A picture becomes a treasured possession just as a beloved book does. For some time now books have been available for young children, but only recently has the worth of pictures been stressed. The picture book has opened up a beautiful new world for the young child.

Children can enjoy pictures before they can read books. Eighteen-month-old Lee keeps his pictures with his books and several times a day he brings them to his mother to "read."

VALUE OF PICTURES FOR CHILDREN

Pictures provide esthetic pleasure for the young child. He delights in the colors and the lovely art form. A beautiful nature scene, within the range of a child's understanding, can stir the emotions and cause him to love God who created nature.

Pictures enlarge the young child's world. Pictures may give him his first knowledge of objects and experiences outside the home. Going from the known to the unknown by way of pictures, he is led into the land of other children and other customs. His curiosity is aroused and the way is open for further information. True, we do not want to force upon him pictures that are beyond his interest, but rather expose him to many pictures that will stimulate his thinking. Pictures can clear up erroneous ideas for the young child. Pictures help children, by way of their imagination, to enter into the experiences of others.

Good pictures help to create an atmosphere for worship. A picture of a little child at prayer suggests giving thanks to God. Charlot Byj's *Bless Us All* and *A Child's Prayer* are excellent for this purpose. For many generations Reynold's *The Infant Samuel at Prayer* has inspired little children to talk to God. One mother placed on her dining room wall a picture of a family giving thanks at the table. As her young child sat in his high chair each day she called attention to the picture. Very soon her son entered into the giving of thanks at mealtime.

Pictures deepen religious concepts. Many children have come to have a warmer love for Jesus because they gazed upon Plockhorst's picture *Suffer Little Children.* A picture of children playing happily together has made right conduct patterns vividly meaningful. Four-year-old Sammy was a little boy who took *what* he wanted, *when* he wanted it. He was continually causing disturbance in the block-building activity. The teacher began to tell stories just for his benefit. From week to week there came encouraging incidents. Attitude was improving. One Sunday the teacher placed on the wall, near the blocks, an attractive picture of children building a tower with blocks. That did it! Sammy became a cooperating member of the block union! Perhaps most teachers have learned the value of pictures in teaching the grace of giving to the young child.

CHOOSING PICTURES FOR THE YOUNG CHILD

At first, the subject matter for the little child's pictures is as limited as his experience. He likes pictures of other children and of animals with which he is familiar. For the very young child the picture should have only one or two large simple objects clearly delineated. There should be little or no background. For this age, pictures should be simple with few details. Too many objects in a picture confuse little children.

After the child has had experience with the one-or-two object picture, he is ready for the picture that tells a story, one with several objects that are related to each other. He is attracted to the realistic picture of action, some experience from everyday life. Symbolism should be avoided. He is literal-minded and his pictures must be of true-to-life, concrete objects. He prefers them colored, with clear tones, if you please.

Pictures of Jesus should be chosen with care; only those that represent Him as a strong, happy person should be used with young children. Margaret was discussing with her adult friend a picture of Jesus found in her Bible storybook. Said she, "I should like to go to heaven . . . I could see how he looked and come back and tell people, so they could paint a real picture of him." [20]

USING PICTURES WITH CHILDREN

Point out familiar objects in the picture. This gets the child's attention and arouses his curiosity. Name the objects and let him find them, thus developing his ability to concentrate and to observe. Use questions to draw out details of the picture.

With the very young child the picture may be used to tell a story. While the little one gazes upon the picture the "storyteller" can talk about the objects and the action of the picture. As children grow older the picture should be used at the conclusion of the story, lest it detract from the verbal picture and eliminate the surprise element of the story. Sometimes, the child will want to "make up" a story about the picture. Pictures may be used for recall when reviewing stories told on previous occasions.

Let the child handle the picture. When he says, "Let me see it," he really means, "Let me feel it." Give him time. Some children perceive details slowly. Pictures should be placed on the child's eye level and he should have freedom to look upon them to his heart's content. In every room where children go, there should be at least one permanent picture. A picture rail in his room provides a place for the pictures that are changed often.

A young child will enjoy a picture collection. Magazine covers and calendars furnish lovely pictures. Help him mount his pictures and provide a box or shelf for them. He will enjoy making a scrapbook with pictures. This is a splendid rainy day project.

Pictures have a silent influence. Truths that young children receive from pictures remain with them through life. They can provide early and lasting impressions for the religious development of the young child.

Teaching Through Music

It is hard to say when the child first becomes interested in music, but it is certain that music has some effect even on a baby. He is a fortunate child who grows up in a home where music is enjoyed.—Garrison and Sheehy[21]

Since the day when little children sang glad hosannas to Jesus as He marched triumphantly into Jerusalem, they have been lifting their voices in praise unto this Friend of Children. Music has a large place in the religious growth of the young child. Through music, the child voices his love, his gratitude, and devotion to God.

VALUES OF MUSIC

Music has a unifying power because it speaks a universal language. Little children as well as older people are drawn closer to each other through the power of group singing.

Singing together draws the family into a closer bond of fellowship. Even the young child will participate, if the songs are on his level. Elizabeth and Eugene had many happy singing experiences sitting on the piano bench with their mother. These singing times began when Elizabeth was only two. When "little brother" came along he joined in.

At first, they did more listening than singing. Soon, however, they joined in with the words. Some of their favorite songs—found in most hymn books—were: "Jesus Loves Me," "Praise Him, All Ye Little Children," and "Jesus Loves the Little Children." At Christmas time, the children chose "Little Baby in the Manger, I Love You," and Luther's "Away in a Manger." As they grew older they learned "Silent Night" and, of course, "Jingle Bells."

From the earliest days they enjoyed Mother Goose songs. They heard them first as lullabies, then they included them in singing time at the piano. Sometimes they made a game of such songs as "Oh, Where, Oh Where Has My Little Dog Gone?" Other songs were added with the years.

Finger-plays gave them much pleasure, also. The very first one, used when Elizabeth was only two months old, was "All for Baby." How her eyes sparkled when she heard, "Here's the way that Baby plays at peek-a-boo!"

Music can be a very vital part of family life. Begin at the beginning, when the baby is tiny. While you have him in your arms, sing to him. Never mind if your voice is not the kind that would make a choir. Your baby will never know it! He feels the warm love and cheer in your voice and he is satisfied. The melody and rhythm appeal to him, too.

Sing as you go about the home chores. It makes the work lighter and the day brighter. Quarreling in the family loses its interest when the melody of a favorite song floats through the house. Try it! It does something for the "singer" as well as for the other members of the family.

Use records with your children; there are some lovely recordings made just for them. Beautiful, soft instrumental music played while the young child sleeps is relaxing and puts him to sleep in a happy frame of mind. Jean Carole's father was a lover of music and had acquired a small, select library of recordings. From the time Jean Carole came home from the hospital, he played records at her sleepy time. He used instrumental music, at first, and introduced "singing" records later.

On her first Christmas, Jean Carole received an album of her own, *Songs for Our Littlest Ones.* At the age of eight months, she responded when they were played. She clapped her hands and "chattered" along with the singing. When she grew older, she played these records for herself.

Music can create a spirit of reverence and worship. This is a good way to begin the family altar time. Quiet instrumental music can provide the atmosphere. Follow this with a song, such as "The Heavenly Father Cares for Me." [22] This can lead into the reading of the Scriptures. In the springtime—or any other time!—you could sing "God's Beautiful World." [23] Well-chosen songs help the child to understand about God. Such songs as "God Is Love" [24] and "God Is Very Near" teach two basic truths about God.

Music can motivate conduct. The Sunday school teacher was having difficulty getting the beginner children to put away their materials. Suddenly she began to sing, "A helper I will be, a helper I will be." Immediately the boys began to put away their blocks, the girls began to straighten up the doll house and a spirit of cooperation pervaded the department room. Mothers find this "works like magic" in the home, too!

Music can provide relaxation for the young child. This is a necessary part of religious instruction. It is physically impossible for children to sit for a long period of time. There must be opportunities for bodily expression. Marches and other instrumental music provide such opportunities. Putting motions to words, such as "The Trees Are Gently Swaying," provide other opportunities. Fingerplays accompanying the singing have been found helpful also. Perhaps it is well to give this precaution here. Never use motions or gestures with worship songs. To do so is to create a spirit of irreverence. Leave the action songs for times of relaxation.

CHOOSING MUSIC FOR THE YOUNG CHILD

Children like songs about things with which they are familiar. Their songs should be short, with much repetition. Symbolism has no place in music for the young child, just as it has no place in his pictures. The language of his songs should be concrete and easily understood. A group of five-year-olds had just sung the chorus "I stand alone on the Word of God, the B—I—B—L—E." A children's worker asked, "What does that mean?" Said John, "It means put your feet on the Bible."

The melody should be of high quality and suited to the words. The notes in the melody should be limited to the staff. The content of his songs should give correct ideas of God, and should inspire right relationships with others. His songs should have beauty of form and literary merit.

TEACHING A NEW SONG

A new song will be introduced when there is a felt need for it. An experience may lead to the remark, "That reminds me of a song." The song may be prefaced by a story, a picture, a bit of nature, or some other appropriate object. The melody could be used on several occasions, so that the refrain will be "humming" in the child's mind. However, at the time the words are introduced it is better to sing without the instrument. In this way the words are more easily understood. Always *sing* the words rather than saying them, thus keeping the words and melody together.

After the words are understood the piano can aid with the melody. If there is no piano let the child sing along with you. The human voice is one of the finest instruments! When the child begins to sing the new song parents must be careful not to sing louder than he. There are two reasons for this: we want the child to sing clearly but not loudly and a child will not sing if he cannot hear his own voice. He seems to say, "Go ahead, you can do the singing for me!"

Pictures help the child to master a new song. He can "read" the pictures and will know what is coming next. Do not try to teach more than one new song at a time. Repeat old songs. The young child enjoys repetition of songs just as he enjoys repetition of stories.

LISTENING MUSIC

The young child's first experience with listening music will likely bring a motor response, such as clapping or skipping. Instrumental music speaks to the child. Mothers have found that a melody on the piano can become a signal to the children. One mother used the C, E, G, C, chord to say: "Chil—dren, come here."

Listening to soft music can bring little children to a time of quiet reverence. Even young children can concentrate briefly as they listen. Their emotions are stirred. From infancy a child should hear good music. Listening to music is a skill that can be cultivated through the years.

Giving young children beautiful music for their "listening pleasure" can make them feel deeply. The right songs planted in the minds and hearts of children can enrich their spiritual lives.

Teaching Through Play

Play is the purest, most spiritual activity of the man at this stage [childhood].—Friedrich Froebel [25]

Play is a dynamic requirement of his physical, mental, and spiritual development.—Hazel Kepler[26]

Constant activity is the law of life in these early years. This restless activity can be directed into channels that promote the little one's religious development. Wholesome, imaginary play—not shooting and killing!—and simple creative activities can provide lessons in character-building.

VALUES OF PLAY

Children learn to cooperate and take turns through group play. They learn to adjust to others. Through play a child comes to understand and sympathize with the other person. Playing with others teaches the child courage, patience, persistence, courtesy, and initiative.

Though it is enjoyable, play is a serious matter to the child. It is the small child's method of learning. In imitative or imaginary play he loses his identity in the object or individual impersonated. Through play he comprehends his environment. It is believed that the emotions are more easily stirred with play and the interest more readily awakened than in any other way. He learns about life. Dramatic or imaginary play is life as he sees it.

Play also is a means of measurement for a child; by it he compares himself with his contemporaries. He learns acceptable ways of working with others. "And be ye kind one to another . . ." (Ephesians 4:32) can bring a vital message to children as they play with others.

A part of each child's day should be spent in solitary play. It has much value for him. Freedom in play with stimulating toys encourages initiative and personality development. The child gains self-confidence and a sense of achievement. His power of concentration grows.

CHOOSING PLAY EQUIPMENT

Choose wisely the child's first toys. They should be durable, washable, and "mouth-proof." Everything he handles will be put in the mouth. He needs few toys during the first year, but they should be the best available.

Do not push him beyond his ability, that only frustrates him. Study your child; let his readiness be your guide. Give him a new toy; if he is not yet ready for it, lay it aside until later.

About the first birthday, children are ready for things that fit together, things they can put together and take apart: lids that stack, a container with a stopper that can be put in and taken out, a large container into which they can drop smaller things. These simple things provide pleasure at an early age. Eleven-month-old Daniel picked up small objects and dropped them into an open-mouthed jar with ease. He fairly delighted in putting them in and then spilling them out again.

When your child comes to the toddler age he can use push-and-pull toys. He likes to drag his toys along with him at this stage. A soft rubber ball, large enough that he can handle, is a joy also. Large peg boards and large blocks are interesting, too.

By the age of two, he begins to be interested in dramatic play. Dolls are important to both boys and girls. Let the little boy have his doll; he will later discard it for more "masculine" toys. He needs to learn the role of father, you know.

Playing "house" is perhaps the most universal "game" of little children. They never tire of it. As the child plays with dolls, some of the truest instincts of manhood and womanhood develop. Four-year-old Susan was so helpful with her baby brother that her mother questioned her, "Where did you learn to talk to little brother and take care of him so well?" Susan answered, "We do that with our baby at kindergarten." Courtesy and table manners can be a direct result of mealtime in the doll home. When your child invites you to tea, you can suggest that "we always say thank you to God before we eat."

Blocks provide many learning experiences. At first the small child seems to move them about just for the sheer fun of it. Later his blocks begin to take form. He may want to build a church house. This is an opportune time to say, "I was glad when they said unto me, let us go into the house of the Lord." Parent and child can talk about the happy things the child does at church.

Little children like to make things. They enjoy creative activities with clay modeling, finger painting, crayola coloring, easel painting, wood-work, and paper construction. All have value for their spiritual growth. Avoid color books. They do not encourage creativeness; they limit the child.

Parents need to keep in mind that the purpose of creative activities is not to produce a finished product nor to develop skill necessarily. The real purpose is what it does for the child. It provides an outlet for expression of personality. The child should have freedom to express life as he sees it, without criticism or correction from adults.

Creative activities furnish relaxation. As the child expresses himself in this type of "play" tensions are released, and satisfaction takes the place of frustration. Art—the expression of some emotion, desire, or impression through the activity of the hands—speaks a language for the young child; it reveals the deep wonderment of life.

Four-year-old Robert made a "Bible." In his "Bible" he wanted his mother to write, "Love one another." "That means love people, children and babies. Pictures in the

Bible, I like them best," said Robert with satisfaction.

Painting offers another art expression. Finger painting can be introduced at an early age. Easel painting is enjoyed by young children, too. Expose your child to the many art media. Experiment with them yourself. They will provide many happy hours of companionship and creative expression.

Parents build a happy comradeship with little children when they play with them. This close companionship opens the way for teaching spiritual truths. In this relaxed atmosphere questions are answered and problems are solved.

Only when parents give of themselves, not merely things, can they mean most to their children. Two little girls were discussing the merits of their mothers. Mary Louise said emphatically, "My mother is the best because she *plays* with me!" Little Katherine had to admit defeat, as she answered sorrowfully, "My mother can't play with me, she's too busy."

Children like to be busy. Parents have the opportunity of providing activities that will not only keep them busy but also promote their religious development. Suggestions are made here with the hope that parents will be stimulated to go afield and explore the possibilities of play. The Suggested Reading list at the end of the book is to help you do just that.

In this chapter, there has been an attempt to show that all the activities of the young child can promote his religious development. All of the arts—storytelling, conversation, pictures, music, and creative art—afford avenues of approach. Perhaps play, that expression of real life to the child, offers the widest opportunity of all.

CHAPTER EIGHT

Together We Teach

The Community

As the baby grows older and reaches out into the neighborhood the influences of the home are strengthened or weakened by his contacts in the community. "Beyond the family the community functions, presenting its heritage to the newcomer." [1]

When parents choose a neighborhood in which to live, consideration should be given to the matter of companions for their children. One father was considering a certain locality for a home, and called on the neighbors surrounding the proposed house to ask how they liked the neighborhood. He inquired about the neighbor's children, the type of recreation available, and the nearest church of his faith. When these questions were satisfactorily answered he decided that it must be a desirable place for his children. The preschool child will be influenced by his immediate environment—his neighbors. Many inconveniences as to location should be cheerfully accepted rather than sacrifice the child's moral welfare.

The activities of the community in which he lives are of extreme importance to the young child. His spiritual welfare is determined, to a large degree, by the moral tone of his neighborhood. The community pattern makes an impression upon his plastic personality. A child who lives in the slum section of a large city does not have the same opportunity for religious development as the child who lives in the open country. The congested areas of cities with their commercialized vice are conducive to moral delinquency, which begins in these early years.

The community must be a fit place for children to live. They cannot be independent of their environment. A toddler begins to assimilate the attitudes of the world outside his family. As he grows older he has a tendency to conform to these attitudes. If children are to develop religiously they must be surrounded by an environment conducive to such growth.

Parents cannot always choose where they live. Sometimes they must live temporarily in an environment that is not best for their children. Christian parents can counteract evil influences surrounding them. Some invite their child's friends into the home for play. (Furniture is easier mended than character!) Others take their children to the nearby park or playground. The hands can be busy while the eyes rest upon the children.

In any community the child may encounter behavior patterns unacceptable to his family. Christian parents must teach their children that there are certain activities their family does not enter into. Always the teaching in the home can be positive: "Our family does it this way; other families must decide their way."

In the community the little child has intimate daily experiences. Here, as he grows older, patterns of conduct are often modified. He begins to imitate the activities of the street and neighborhood. Jimmy was a friendly, lovable three-year-old when his parents moved into a congested housing project. One morning he climbed to the upstairs apartment with a bloody nose and a torn shirt. He was in high glee. Said he, "Now, I'm somebody, 'cause I can fight like the big boys!"

A child needs to have a sense of belonging in his community. In his mind, his neighborhood is associated with home. Parents should interpret the activities of his community for him, and should teach gratitude for the helpers of that community. He can be led to feel a responsibility for his neighborhood and to take a pride in it, as he participates in its activities. He should be led cheerfully and lovingly to help the less fortunate around him. He can be led to understand and to appreciate the people in whose midst he lives.

The Church

Churches are the greatest stabilizing force in any community. "The family needs the co-operation of the church in its task of developing religious lives." [2]

The church, too, makes an important contribution to the little child. One of the objectives in the religious development of the child is to create a love for the church. Although the church can never be a substitute for the home, it has something to offer that the child cannot receive elsewhere. The atmosphere of worship and the spirit of fellowship found in some churches cannot be duplicated.

THE CHURCH MINISTERING TO THE CHILD

Many opportunities for learning about God are offered by the church through the Sunday school on Sunday morning, the training organization on Sunday night, the worship services, the missionary meeting during the week, and the vacation Bible school in the summertime. Many churches are providing an extended program in which the activities of the Sunday school and training organization are continued for the little children who do not yet attend the worship services in the auditorium.

Every phase of his church life should be committed to the child's religious development. The church leaders and teachers seek to make the Christian religion meaningful to the young child and vital to his daily living, through the use of the Bible, stories, nature study, conversation, music, pictures, play and creative activities. These early church experiences lay the foundation for the time when the little child will come to know Jesus as his personal Saviour.

Lives are changed under the influence of the church. Raymond started Sunday school at the age of four. He was a problem to the teachers and to the other children. After four years of patient guidance and careful teaching, his mother came to his teacher to express gratitude for what the church school had meant to her boy. She reported this conversation: " 'One day he came to me, and said, "Mother, I wish I could love as much as God does." "Why," I said, "don't you love Daddy, Mother, little sister and brother?" "Yes," he said, "and lots more besides, but I can't give them trees, birds, flowers, rain, and nice teachers who don't get mad with them when they're bad." ' "[3]

Many parents believe that attendance at the worship service is essential to the religious development of the little child. The association with church people, the atmosphere of reverence, the message of song and sermon have moral values for him.

THE CHURCH MINISTERING TO THE HOME

The biggest thing that the church can do for the religious help of children is to reach, instruct, and inspire the parents at home to fulfill their God-given mission to the children. The church begins this part of her work when it leads unsaved parents to Christ. It accomplishes a still more difficult part when it leads the same parents to make their home a real religious training School for the children. The home and the church must be brought into a more general, a closer, and more hearty cooperation.[4]

Visitation in the home can bring the family and the church into closer relationship and secure the cooperation of parents in the church's ministry to the children. Many parents are eager for that fellowship and for guidance in their problems with children. Sometimes unsaved parents are reached through the children. The slogan of the Cradle Roll department of one denomination is "A Christian home for every baby." No higher goal could be set for the homes of all little children.

The School

Some churches are beginning to realize the value of the day nursery school and kindergarten. The demand for teachers in these schools far exceeds the supply. Churches know that if they would build for the future they must begin with the little child today.

Many public nursery school and kindergarten teachers are alert to their opportunities for the religious development of the children. The day school has the little child for a longer period of time and thus can have greater opportunities for laying the foundation of the child's religious life than does the Sunday school. If the Christian teacher gains the confidence and love of her children, she lays the foundation for religion. She can influence the little child for God, whether or not she does any formal teaching of religion.

In the early days of America the public school was considered an agency for character education. Much of the textbook material was taken from the Bible. Today, the Bible cannot be taught in public schools, but character-education can and should be continued.

The greatest single factor in the nursery school and in the kindergarten is the teacher. Her life is far more impressive than anything she teaches. Her pupils sense her attitude toward the things of God. If Christianity means much to her it will be attractive to them.

Association with other children in the public nursery school and kindergarten is another factor in character-building. Children can learn unselfishness and consideration for others in these real life experiences. Here they learn to take responsibility for their own actions as they live in a world of their contemporaries. Children accept as routine good habit patterns much more readily in a group where all cheerfully work together.

Experiences of living in a group, under the guidance of Christian teachers, can be vital to the religious development of the child. Friendly attitudes and good habits that will influence all the future can become fixed. The little child's life can be enriched by sharing experiences of wonder and reverence with the group as he participates in nature study. Religious interpretations can be given to the child's contacts with others.

It is often easier for nursery school or kindergarten

teachers to see a child's problems objectively than for his parents. Parents are so closely bound to their children by emotional ties that it is difficult for them to see these little people as others see them. Children need this unprejudiced judgment of personalities outside the home.

Through the darkness of moral, social, and economic upheaval today there comes a ray of light, generated by the awakened interest of the public school in character education. School teachers are attacking vigorously the momentous task of changing lives that come to them for instruction. The state is being aroused to its responsibility. The public school must contribute to the moral integration of these future citizens. Too long the task has been relegated to the homes and to the church. With new and improved methods our public schools must return to the first purposes and principles for which they were organized. Teachers who realize that the mental and spiritual health of the little child are closely related are making a great contribution to the religious development of the children in their schools.

The adult world owes a debt to the children, to so guide in their religious development that they may be confident persons who can live happily with others. The home, the community, the church, and the school must unite in their moral and spiritual nurture to the end that the foundations of life may be secure for the future. Every child has a right to know God and it is our high privilege and solemn obligation to introduce him to the Father during these early, formative years.

The urgency of the task presents a challenge. What is done for the young child will determine the future of the home, the community, the nation, and the world.

We turn to the oncoming generation of children with hope and concern. We of their adult world have a grave responsibility in helping them to strengthen the foundations for secure and confident living and in developing their capacities to live with others. Patience and energy are needed to search out and find ways to endow them with the moral and spiritual training which is their fundamental heritage.[5]

Notes

CHAPTER ONE

1. James L. Hymes, Jr., *Understanding Your Child* (New York, Prentice-Hall, Inc., 1954), p. 184.
2. Mrs. W. C. Morgan, "Mom-mie, I Wanta Talk to God," *Home Life* (April, 1949).
3. Benjamin Spock, *The Pocket Book of Baby and Child Care* (New York, Pocket Books, Inc., 1955), p. 460.

CHAPTER TWO

1. Steuart Henderson Britt, *Social Psychology of Modern Life* (New York, Rinehart & Company, Inc., 1941), p. 313.
2. Gladys Gardner Jenkins, Helen Shacter and William W. Bauer, *These Are Your Children* (Chicago, Scott, Foresman and Company, 1953), p. 6.
3. Anna W. M. Wolf, *The Parents' Manual* (New York, Simon & Schuster, Inc., 1947), pp. 12-13.
4. Ruth Strang, *An Introduction to Child Study* (New York, The Macmillan Company, 3d ed., 1952), p. 50.
5. Louise Woodcock, *Life and Ways of the Two-Year-Old* (New York, Basic Books, Inc., 1941).
6. *Ibid.*, p. 16.
7. *Ibid.*, pp. 216-217.
8. Strang, *loc. cit.*
9. Anna Botsford Comstock, *Handbook of Nature Study* (Ithaca, N. Y., Comstock Publishing Associates, 24th ed., 1957).
10. Benjamin Spock, *The Pocket Book of Baby and Child Care* (New York, Pocket Books, Inc., 1955), p. 281.

CHAPTER THREE

1. Arthur Jersild, *Child Psychology* (New York, Prentice-Hall, Inc., 1955), p. 478.
2. James L. Hymes, Jr., *Understanding Your Child* (New York, Prentice-Hall, Inc., 1954), p. 20.
3. Clarence H. Benson, *An Introduction to Child Study* (Chicago, The Bible Institute Colportage Assoc., 1927), p. 113.

CHAPTER FOUR

1. James L. Hymes, Jr., *A Child Development Point of View* (Englewood Cliffs, N. J., Prentice-Hall, Inc., 1956), p. 33.
2. Gladys Gardner Jenkins, Helen Shacter, and William W. Bauer, *These Are Your Children* (Chicago, Scott, Foresman and Company, 1953), p. 226.
3. Benjamin Spock, *The Pocket Book of Baby and Child Care* (New York, Pocket Books, Inc., 1955), p. 246.
4. Ruth Strang, *An Introduction to Child Study* (New York, The Macmillan Company, 3d ed., 1952), p. 119.
5. Catherine Stern and Toni S. Gould, *The Early Years of Childhood* (New York, Harper & Brothers, 1955), p. 156.
6. William E. Blatz and Helen Bott, *Parents and the Preschool Child* (New York, William Morrow & Company, 1929), pp. 231-232.
7. *Ibid.*, p. 59.
8. Stern and Gould, *op. cit.*, p. 165.
9. *Ibid.*, p. 26.
10. Arthur Jersild, *Child Psychology* (New York, Prentice-Hall, Inc., 1955), p. 396.

CHAPTER FIVE

1. Douglas A. Thom, *Everyday Problems of the Everyday Child* (New York, D. Appleton-Century Co., Inc., 1927), p. 151.
2. Arthur Jersild, *Child Psychology* (New York, Prentice-Hall, Inc., 1955), p. 343.
3. Frances McKinnon Morton, *First Steps in Religious Education* (Nashville, Tenn., Cokesbury Press, 1930), p. 145.

4. George Stewart, *Can I Teach My Child Religion?* (New York, Harper & Brothers, 1933), p. 89.
5. William E. Blatz and Helen Bott, *Parents and the Preschool Child* (New York, William Morrow & Company, 1929), p. 157.
6. Karl de Schweinitz, *Growing Up* (New York, The Macmillan Company, 3d ed., 1954).
7. Gladys Gardner Jenkins, Helen Shacter, and William W. Bauer, *These Are Your Children* (Chicago, Scott, Foresman and Company, 1953), p. 264.
8. Stewart, *op. cit.*, p. 132.

CHAPTER SIX

1. Paul H. Vieth, *Objectives in Religious Education* (New York, Harper & Brothers, 1930), p. 18.
2. John Milton Price (editor), *Introduction to Religious Education* (New York, The Macmillan Company, 1932), p. 22.
3. A. J. William Myers, *Religion for Today* (New York, Association Press, 1941), p. 36.
4. John Milton Price, *op. cit.*, p. 27.
5. Dora P. Chaplin, *Children and Religion* (New York, Charles Scribner's Sons, 1945), p. 28.
6. Mrs. H. A. Deckert, "Summertime with God," *Children's Religion* (June, 1948).
7. Frances Weld Danielson, *Lessons for Teacher of Beginners* (Boston, The Pilgrim Press, 1914), p. 28.
8. Lewis Joseph Sherrill, *The Opening Doors of Childhood* (New York, The Macmillan Company, 1939), p. 29.
9. Sallie Rust Moss, *Give Your Child a Chance* (Nashville, Tenn., Broadman Press, 1938), p. 62.
10. Robbie Trent, *Your Child and God* (New York, Harper & Brothers, rev. ed., 1952), p. 44.
11. Anna Freelove Betts, *The Mother-Teacher of Religion* (New York, The Abingdon Press, 1922), p. 92.
12. Trent, *op. cit.*, p. 89.
13. Edith E. Read Mumford, *How We Can Help Children to Pray* (London, Longmans, Green & Company, 1923), p. 19.
14. Francis L. Strickland, *Psychology of Religious Experience* (New York, The Abingdon Press, 1924), p. 222.
15. Clarence H. Benson, *An Introduction to Child Study* (Chicago, The Bible Institute Colportage Assoc., 1927), p. 117.

16. Herman J. Sweet, *Opening the Door for God* (Philadelphia, The Westminster Press, 1943), p. 66.
17. Sherrill, *op. cit.*, p. 75.
18. Pauline Hargis, "My Bible Book," *Beginner Teacher* (January, February, March, 1949).
19. H. Clay Trumbull, *Hints on Child-Training* (Philadelphia, The Sunday School Times Company, 1925), p. 145.
20. Aurora Medford Shumate, *Songs for the Preschool Age* (Nashville, Tenn., Broadman Press, 1947), p. 17.

CHAPTER SEVEN

1. John Milton Gregory, *The Seven Laws of Teaching* (Grand Rapids, Mich., Baker Book House, 1956), p. 2.
2. Anna Botsford Comstock, *Handbook of Nature Study* (Ithaca, N. Y., Comstock Publishing Associates, 24th ed., 1957), p. 3.
3. Aurora Medford Shumate, *Songs for the Preschool Age* (Nashville, Tenn., Broadman Press, 1947), p. 22.
4. Claudia Royal, *Storytelling* (Nashville, Tenn., Broadman Press, 1955), p. 91.
5. Mrs. J. B. Burton, "Bible Study in the Home Supplementing Bible Teaching in the Sunday School," *The Sunday School Builder* (February, 1949).
6. Royal, *op. cit.*, pp. 25-26.
7. Robbie Trent, *Your Child and God* (New York, Harper & Brothers, rev. ed., 1952), p. 68.
8. Royal, *op. cit.*, p. 93.
9. Lucy Sprague Mitchell, *Here and Now Story Book* (New York, E. P. Dutton & Co., Inc., rev. ed., 1948), p. 124.
10. Edward Porter St. John, *Stories and Story-Telling* (New York, The Abingdon Press, rev. ed., 1910-1918), p. 1.
11. Annis Duff, *Bequest of Wings* (New York, Viking Press, Inc., 1954), p. 23.
12. May Hill Arbuthnot, *Children and Books* (Chicago, Scott, Foresman and Company, 1947), pp. 2-9.
13. *Ibid.*, pp. 34-39.
14. Duff, *loc. cit.*
15. Arbuthnot, *op. cit.*, p. 2.
16. Mary M. Thomson, *Talk It Out With Your Child* (New York, McGraw-Hill Book Company, Inc., 1953), p. 5.
17. Trent, *op. cit.*, p. 142.

18. Orabelle C. Jones, *The Nursery Department of the Sunday School* (Nashville, Tenn., The Sunday School Board of the Southern Baptist Convention, 1946), p. 85.
19. Pauline Hargis, *Teaching the Beginner Child* (Nashville, Tenn., The Sunday School Board of the Southern Baptist Convention, 1948), p. 63.
20. Elizabeth McEwen Shields, *Guiding the Little Child* (Nashville, Tenn., Broadman Press, 1936), p. 103.
21. Charlotte Gano Garrison and Emma Dickson Sheehy, *At Home With Children* (New York, Henry Holt & Company, Inc., rev. ed., 1949), p. 139.
22. Shumate, *op. cit.*, p. 16.
23. Mattie C. Leatherwood, *Songs We Sing* (Nashville, Tenn., Broadman Press, 1939), p. 33.
24. Shumate, *op. cit.*, p. 20.
25. Friedrich Froebel, quoted by F. N. Painter, *A History of Education* (New York, D. Appleton and Co., 1909), p. 310.
26. Hazel Kepler, *The Child and His Play* (New York, Funk & Wagnalls Company, 1952), p. v.

CHAPTER EIGHT

1. Stewart G. Cole, *Character and Christian Education* (Nashville, Tenn., Cokesbury Press, 1936), p. 40.
2. Henry F. Cope, *Religious Education in the Family* (Chicago, The University of Chicago Press, 1917), p. 201.
3. Lewis Joseph Sherrill, *The Opening Doors of Childhood* (New York, The Macmillan Company, 1939), pp. 154-55.
4. Rev. William George Koons, *The Child's Religious Life* (New York, Eaton & Mains, 1903), p. 17.
5. "Toward a 1950 White House Conference on Children and Youth," pamphlet, developed by Conference on State Planning for Children and Youth, March 30-April 1, 1948, Federal Security Agency, Social Security Administration, Children's Bureau, p. 2.

Suggested Reading

CHAPTER ONE

Robert A. Lapsley, Jr., *Beside the Hearthstone* (Richmond, Va., John Knox Press, 1953). An inspiring book for Christian parents, with emphasis upon the home. The author discusses the school, the church, the Sabbath, the Bible, prayer, religion and many other topics as they relate to the home.

Sallie Rust Moss, *Give Your Child a Chance* (Nashville, Tenn., Broadman Press, 1938). Although much of this book has to do with the school-age child, its message is to mothers of little children as well. The author points to the Bible as a guide for parents and children.

Herman J. Sweet, *Opening the Door for God* (Philadelphia, Westminster Press, 1943). This book offers guidance and inspiration to parents in the religious nurture of their children.

Robbie Trent, *Your Child and God* (New York, Harper & Brothers, rev. ed., 1952). For all who work with children Miss Trent raises a profound question: Shall we teach them about God? If so, how? She challenges our thinking as to the importance of early training. Because of her emphasis on the home, the book should be read by every parent as well as church worker.

CHAPTER TWO

C. Anderson and Mary M. Aldrich, *Babies Are Human Beings* (New York, The Macmillan Company, 1954). A delightful book for parents (as well as teachers), giving an interpretation of the natural development of young children. The authors show that each child has a distinct personality at the age of one day! They give a sane philosophy of baby-parent relationships. Charming baby photographs illustrate the book.

Arnold Gesell and Frances L. Ilg, *Infant and Child in the Culture of Today* (New York, Harper & Brothers, 1943). In collaboration with others, Dr. Gesell, the eminent authority on children, has given us a very helpful guide for the first five years of life. The authors discuss the mental growth characteristics of early childhood, with special attention to individual variations.

Gladys Gardner Jenkins, Helen Shacter and William W. Bauer, *These Are Your Children* (Chicago, Scott, Foresman and Company, 1953). This book discusses the physical, mental, social and emotional development of each age group from infancy through adolescence. Pen pictures give accounts of individual children at each age level. The home and parents' part in the family life are stressed. Aids for studying children are offered at the close of the book. Any parent would do well to read this book and keep it for ready reference.

Benjamin Spock and John Reinhart, *A Baby's First Year* (New York, Duell, Sloan and Pearce, 1955). A delightful book, with full page close-up photographs. A warm, day by day account of the baby's first year. Interesting and inspiring reading!

Ruth Strang, *An Introduction to Child Study* (New York, The Macmillan Company, 3d ed., 1952). The first thirteen chapters discuss early childhood. The author recognizes the importance of the family, "with emphasis on the potentialities of parents rather than on their faults."

Louise Woodcock, *Life and Ways of the Two-Year-Old* (New York, Basic Books, Inc., 1952). A charming description of two-year-olds. A record of a teacher who understands her children. There are episodes from everyday life to illustrate the ways of this age.

CHAPTER THREE

Frances Dunlap Heron, *Kathy Ann Kindergartner* (Nashville, Tenn., Abingdon Press, 1945). The author writes out of her experience as a mother of four children, each of whom "contributed some characteristic or incident to this book." Kathy Ann tells of experiences as seen through the eyes of a five-year-old.

Margaret Lee Runbeck, *Our Miss Boo* (New York, Appleton-Century-Crofts, Inc., 1942). Miss Boo is an entrancing child beloved by all who meet her. All the delightful adventures of early childhood are given from a "child's-eye view."

CHAPTER FOUR

William E. Blatz and Helen Bott, *Parents and the Preschool Child* (New York, William Morrow & Co., 1944). The authors have had experience with children and their parents. Their book "aims to point out ways and means of avoiding the pitfalls that lie in the way of every normal child in the course of his social adjustments." Their main emphasis is upon "prevention rather than cure."

James L. Hymes, Jr., *A Child Development Point of View* (Englewood Cliffs, N. J., Prentice-Hall, Inc., 1956). This is a book aimed at teachers but it has much to offer parents of young children. This popular author stresses the preventive side of mental health. His aim is to "build good feeling into children."

Arthur Jersild, *Child Psychology* (New York, Prentice-Hall, Inc., 1955). This book deals with "both the internal and the external dimensions of a child's world." Written for the classroom as well as for the home.

Benjamin Spock, *The Pocket Book of Baby and Child Care* (New York, Pocket Books, Inc., 1955). A common-sense guide to parents. The kindliness of the author shows through. Very readable and very encouraging. The complete index makes it a book for ready reference.

Catherine Stern and Toni S. Gould, *The Early Years of Childhood* (New York, Harper & Brothers, 1955). The authors advocate "education through insight." They take a middle-of-the-road course between the arbitrary "authoritarian" approach and "unrestrained permissiveness." The illustrations from the Castle School are most helpful. Mother and daughter have produced a book for the encouragement of other parents.

CHAPTER FIVE

Rhoda M. Bacmeister, *Caring for the Runabout Child* (New York, E. P. Dutton & Co., 1937). A guide for the two- to six-year-old, the author writes out of her experience as a mother and nursery school teacher. A helpful book for parents of young children.

Irma Simonton Black, *Off to a Good Start* (New York, Harcourt, Brace & Company, Inc., 1953). The author shows a real appreciation for parents. Says she, "Being a good parent is a tough, demanding job." With this attitude, she writes a handbook to guide them on their way. A helpful book.

Smiley and Margaret Gray Blanton, *Child Guidance* (New York, Appleton-Century-Crofts, Inc., 1927). This is a practical book about healthy, normal children. The authors have written for parents "who in order to make the most of their children's lives must have sympathetic guidance and understanding." They make a study of the causes of behavior and offer suggestions for leading each individual child to realize his greatest potentialities.

Herman N. Bundesen, *The Baby Manual* (New York, Simon & Schuster, Inc., 1944). Book One discusses prenatal care; Book Two, the care of the baby; Book Three, the premature baby; Book Four, the first two years. The question and answer method makes this a good book for ready reference.

Child Study Association of America, *Parents' Questions* (New York, Harper & Brothers, rev. ed., 1947). This book by the staff of the Child Study Association grew out of their experience with parents and children. It deals with behavior problems of children and answers "the everyday questions of worried parents." Case studies illustrate ways of dealing with children.

Marie Hall Ets, *The Story of a Baby* (New York, Viking Press, Inc., 1951). A charming book. It pictures the growth of a baby from "a life too small to be seen at all," through its many stages until the baby's birth. This book provides a happy way of introducing to the young child the facts about life.

Sidonie Matsner Gruenberg (editor), *The Encyclopedia of Child Care and Guidance* (Garden City, L. I., Doubleday & Company, Inc., 1954). A complete guide for parents and grandparents. The book has a thumb index and offers help for the understanding of all ages.

Leslie B. Hohman, *As the Twig Is Bent* (New York, The Macmillan Company, 1954). A sound, practical guide for parents. This physician's point of view is refreshing and down-to-earth. He directs the reader's attention to "character formation" and "habit building."

James L. Hymes, Jr., *Understanding Your Child* (New York, Prentice-Hall, Inc., 1954). A very human book from a noted educator. The author shows a sympathetic understanding of children but he also sees the parents' viewpoint. You will enjoy the forthright style of the author and profit from the practical suggestions.

Frances L. Ilg and Louise Bates Ames, *Child Behavior* (New York, Harper & Brothers, 1955). Specific suggestions are given about behavior problems of children. Causes and cure are mentioned concerning each problem. The book comes from the Gesell Institute of Child Development.

Gladys Gardner Jenkins, Harry Orrin Gillett, Edward H. Stullken and Martha Bennett King, *Child Training* (Lake Bluff, Ill., Child Development, Inc., 1956). As its title claims, this is a guide to successful parenthood. The book describes the child from birth through age sixteen. Emphasis is given to parents and their part in building a happy family.

Julia M. Long, *How to Help the Baby Grow* (New York, Greenberg, Publisher, Inc., 1955). A delightfully illustrated guide for parents and baby sitters. Simply written and very practical. At the close, there is a code and a quiz for baby sitters.

Donald M. Maynard, *Your Home Can Be Christian* (Nashville, Tenn., Abingdon-Cokesbury Press, 1952). Dr. Maynard deals realistically with the problems of today. He shows how they can be handled in a Christian way. He discusses such problems as eating, sleeping, getting along with other children, discipline, fear, telling falsehoods, sex education, and others common to young children. A warmhearted, practical book for parents who want to build happy, Christian homes "where Christian character is formed and the Christian faith is a wholesome, natural part of family living."

Wava McCullough, *Child Care* (New York, McGraw-Hill Book Company, Inc., 1954). This is an illustrated handbook of child care, from birth to six years. A unique book written to "serve as a guide in the everyday care of the child." More than 400 illustrations make the book a pleasure to read!

Emily Post, *Children Are People* (New York, Funk & Wagnalls Company, 1940). A warm and understanding book that will bring you closer to your child. The author shows rare insight and wisdom.

Martha May Reynolds, *Children From Seed to Saplings* (New York, McGraw-Hill Book Company, Inc., 1939). The author discusses the growth of children, physically, mentally, and emotionally, beginning with infancy.

Frank Howard Richardson, *How to Get Along With Children* (Atlanta, Tupper and Love, 1954). "This book is rich with sensible answers to the questions parents of every generation ask." The author begins with infancy and goes to adolescence. He raises a question and then answers it. A choice book for parents.

Karl de Schweinitz, *Growing Up* (New York, The Macmillan Company, 3d ed., 1954). A wholesome book to use with the child as soon as he begins to ask questions. Beautifully illustrated. After a quarter-century it remains a popular book.

Irene Schumo Seipt, *Your Child's Happiness* (Cleveland, The World Publishing Company, 1955). Out of her experience as a parent and teacher, the author offers help to other parents. Her viewpoint is that life with children can be a real adventure.

Maxwell S. Stewart, *The Growing Family* (New York, Harper & Brothers, 1955). Many noted people contributed to this book. Among others are James L. Hymes, Jr., Dorothy Baruch, and Clara Lambert. Their emphasis is the unity of the family.

Douglas A. Thom, *Everyday Problems of the Everyday Child* (New York, D. Appleton-Century Co., Inc., 1927). Written many years ago, this book is still helpful to parents today.

Wilfred and Frances Tyler, *The Little World of Home* (Nashville, Tenn., Broadman Press, 1950). This husband and wife team have given us wise counsel for rearing children in a Christian environment. They write out of their experience as parents. Especially helpful for young people—married or about-to-be-married.

Ruth Wendell Washburn, *Children Have Their Reasons* (New York, Appleton-Century-Crofts, Inc., 1942). Dr. Washburn has written out of her fifteen years of experience at the Clinic of Child Development at Yale University. She places a high value on parenthood, speaking of it as "first of the professions." There is a reverence for life in its pages. Reading the book gives you a warm feeling and the thought, "I'm glad I'm a parent!"

Regina H. Westcott, *Does Your Child Obey?* (New York, Harper & Brothers, 1943). The author raises the question "What's the good of obedience?" Then she discusses ways and means of encouraging the right sort of obedience.

Anna W. M. Wolf, *The Parents' Manual* (New York, Simon & Schuster, Inc., 1947). The author writes out of her experience of counseling for the Child Study Association. She discusses the problems of children and then devotes a chapter to "problem parents." Her chapter on "Things to Make and Do" is most helpful!

Anna W. M. Wolf and Suzanne Szasz, *Helping Your Child's Emotional Growth* (Garden City, L. I., Doubleday & Company, Inc., 1954). "This book is reassuring." The author offers a very practical, common-sense guide to parents. The photographs, many of them full page spread, add much to the interest of the book. You'll want to read it!

John Charles Wynn, *How Christian Parents Face Family Problems* (Philadelphia, The Westminster Press, 1954). A gem of a book for all parents who want the best for their children. The chapters: Discipline, Family Worship, Parental Patience, Sex, and the Handicapped Child should prove especially helpful to the parents of young children.

CHAPTER SIX

Billy Graham, *Peace with God* (New York, Permabooks, 1955). In his forthright manner, Billy Graham opens up to the seeking soul the way to God. As he says, "This book has been written for the man in the street." He makes the way very plain.

Pauline Hargis and others, *Teaching the Beginner Child* (Nashville, Tenn., The Sunday School Board of the Southern Baptist Convention, 1948). A splendid book on teaching religion to the four- and five-year-old child. There is a chapter on the child and several chapters on methods of teaching him.

Georgia Harkness, *Prayer and the Common Life* (Nashville, Tenn., Abingdon-Cokesbury Press, 1948). The author presents a sane, sensible discussion of prayer in the work-a-day world. She reviews hindrances to prayer, ways of praying and the fruits of prayer. A book to stimulate prayer life.

Orabelle C. Jones, *The Nursery Department of the Sunday School* (Nashville, Tenn., The Sunday School Board of the Southern Baptist Convention, rev. ed., 1954). Mrs. Jones covers briefly the entire field of Sunday nursery school education: relationships, the nursery child, organization, equipment, methods, and problems, and gives a picture of a helpful guide to all those who work with nursery-age children.

Eugenia Price, *The Burden Is Light* (Westwood, N. J., Fleming H. Revell Company, 1955). "The autobiography of a transformed pagan who took God at His Word." Eugenia Price was a successful radio script writer leading a life of empty sinfulness. Then, one night, "in a lonely hotel room high above New York City" she met God. She tells of the transformation from atheism to a "newly born child of Christ." This pilgrim writer inspires other pilgrims along the way.

Dale Evans Rogers, *My Spiritual Diary* (Westwood, N. J., Fleming H. Revell Company, 1955). "This is an intimate, honest, humble accounting of one soul to its Creator." This famous movie star tells of her defeats and final victory in her climb toward God. A most inspiring book!

Hannah Whitall Smith, *The Christian's Secret of a Happy Life* (Westwood, N. J., Fleming H. Revell Company, 1952). An old book with ever new inspiration. The author discusses the difficulties confronting the Christian way of life and suggests ways of victory over them.

CHAPTER SEVEN

Rose H. Alschuler and associates, *Two to Six* (New York, William Morrow & Company, rev. ed., 1947). Habits, books, stories, music, play materials, nature, and excursions are discussed.

Rose H. Alschuler (editor), *Children's Centers* (New York, William Morrow & Company, 1947). Drawings and specifications for play equipment.

May Hill Arbuthnot, *Children and Books* (Chicago, Scott, Foresman and Company, 1947). An expert guide on children's literature.

May Hill Arbuthnot, *Time for Poetry* (Chicago, Scott, Foresman and Company, 1952). "A complete library of poems for children 4 to 14."

Anna Botsford Comstock, *Handbook of Nature Study* (Ithaca, N. Y., Comstock Publishing Associates, 24th ed., 1957). Every phase of nature study is presented with attractive up-to-date pictures from real life. A complete guide.

Annis Duff, *Bequest of Wings* (New York, Viking Press, Inc., 1954). A family's adventure with books. An inspiring book.

Lillian and Godfrey Frankel, *What to Do with Your Preschooler* (New York, Sterling Publishing Co., 1953). Doug Anderson's humorous drawings add spice to this delightful guide. The authors suggest "enjoyable activities for children 2 to 5 years old."

Charlotte Gano Garrison and Emma Dickson Sheehy, *At Home With Children* (New York, Henry Holt & Company, 1943). This is "a guide to preschool play and training." Brief and practical.

Kenneth Graham, *The Wind in the Willows* (New York, Charles Scribner's Sons, 1953). Charming stories to read or tell.

Sidonie Matsner Gruenberg, *Favorite Stories Old and New* (Garden City, L. I., Doubleday & Company, Inc., 1942). Mrs. Gruenberg's book grew out of her experience with her four children.

Francis R. Horwich and Reinald Werrenrath, Jr., *Have Fun With Your Children* (New York, Prentice-Hall, Inc., 1954). "Miss Frances" of "Ding Dong School" gives practical suggestions for meeting prevalent problems. There are many ideas for activities.

A. A. Milne, *When We Were Very Young* (New York, E. P. Dutton & Co., Inc., 1945). A "straight to the heart" book of "child-verses." This makes delightful reading for the grown-up as well as the small child!

Lucy Sprague Mitchell, *Here and Now Story Book* (New York, E. P. Dutton & Co., 1948). Stories of everyday life for the two- through seven-year-olds. These stories are especially adapted to "telling."

Hilary Page, *Playtime in the First Five Years* (New York, J. B. Lippincott Company, 1954). Activities for the young child, from infancy.

Emilie Poulsson, *Finger Plays* (New York, Lothrop, Lee & Shepard Co., Inc., 1893). From three months on, these can be used with young children.

Claudia Royal, *Storytelling* (Nashville, Tenn., Broadman Press, 1955). The author points out the values of storytelling for spiritual growth. Among others, there are chapters on: choosing the story, preparing the story, telling the story, and dramatizing the story.

Marguerita Rudolph, *Living and Learning in Nursery School* (New York, Harper and Brothers, 1954). An interesting picture of life in a nursery school. Mrs. Rudolph shows how little children react to the nursery school teacher. Helpful to parents because many of the methods may be adapted to the home.

Ruth Sawyer, *The Way of the Storyteller* (New York, Viking Press, Inc., 1947). This should give you an appreciation for the art and possibilities of storytelling. Spiritual values are pointed out.

Aurora Medford Shumate, *Songs for the Preschool Age* (Nashville, Tenn., Broadman Press, 1947). Lovely little songs that teach about God. Spiritual truths, in the child's language, are set to beautiful music, in the child's range.